Cascade

Better practices for effective delivery of information systems in a multi-project environment. ©

David W. Wright

First Edition, 2008

Published by Lulu.com

ISBN: 978-1-4357-1853-1

Kelso, to Kelso's Dad: Did you make the graph?

Kelso's Dad: I wish!

...from "That 70's Show"

Table of Contents

INTRODUCTION

This book is written for people who work at companies that have an IT department to support their non-IT business. In comparison, this book is not written for people who work at IT companies, from Google on down to someone selling excel macros. The main reason is that I have not worked for an IT company and, although I have worked with many in customer-vendor relationships, I do not feel qualified to write about something I do not have experience with. However, even companies selling IT need some other IT to help run their business, so perhaps some of my experiences may overlap with theirs.

Given that, let us consider the vast majority of companies that are making automobiles or serving hamburgers or providing investment advice or any and everything else. In those companies you will find a department/division filled with IT 'professionals': Programmers, Project Managers, Analysts, Testers, Implementers, Operators, and loads of other specialists like Database Administrators and Network Engineers. (I use *professional* in quotes because long-standing professions like lawyers and engineers like to protect the use of the word.)

The name of this group has evolved generally to the 'Information Technology Department', or IT for short (no 'D' at the end); such past names as "Data Processing" or "Management Information Systems" seem to have faded away. As an acronym, "IT" is used interchangeably to name the department and describe the functional scope addressed by that department.

So, as we speed through the first decade of the 21st century and on into the next, what is the common situation that these IT departments face?

- It probably includes an installed set of information systems that are used by the business to control and report on its operations. There is always more than just one system, and possibly hundreds, many doing the same work as many others. Some may be decades-old, a few may be recent and using fairly new technologies, with the implementations of the rest spread-out over the history of the department since that first 'computing machine' was purchased, with the wide range of development and operating technologies which that implies. (How along ago did you read that your mainframe computer was dead? Did it die? Not likely.) The still favourite term for describing this installed base is *legacy systems.*

- It probably includes a large back-log of requested changes to that installed base of systems, overlaid with a long list of problems/bugs in the systems that the business is currently 'working around' until they ever get fixed.

- It probably includes an "IT Strategy" that describes in glowing terms how the above two cases will be remedied by moving to some new method or tool or one enterprise system… if the budget and resources can ever be freed up from fixing and changing the current systems.

- It is probably overseen by a senior management group (or steering committee or review board) that is charged with deciding what IT work is approved and carried out. This group may be formal or informal, and may only be one person in the end, the CEO or someone he/she has delegated it to; since IT costs money, the CFO is a common choice.

    In this structure, the head of the IT department (CIO is the hot title, of course) plays a committee secretary and/or facilitator role, who is supposed to assist the rest of management in making their IT choices. This is a difficult role, as the rest of management has a split-view of IT, that most of it is a waste of time and money, except for the work each one wants for their own department/division.[1]

---

[1] There was a movement in the 80's and 90's to decentralize IT, give a sub-set of the IT staff to each department and division to work exclusively on that area's projects. It sounded good, of course, until each business VP found out they had to manage techie IT

- There are probably a large number of current projects being carried out, that no one can remember when they started and, even if some target date has been set, no reasonable expectation exists that they will end soon.

- It is peopled by a group of IT staff that has remained the same size in numbers, or has been reduced, while being charged with doing more work than ever: "Work Smart, Not Hard", "Do More With Less". Each person is probably assigned to many of those current projects, juggling the work and trying to determine what they should really be working on.

    The overall morale and effectiveness of this staff depends greatly on the skills of their immediate management and more senior managers who provide some level of inspiration; if not, morale plunges and turnover increases.

Sound familiar? Then you have the same experiences as me, and I have written this book for you.

The premise of this book is that the situation described above *can* change, but it is usually slow-going; or worse, there can be an immediate change when your department is outsourced. In the meantime, what can be done to be "successful" in your average IT department in your average company?[2]

What has to be done is to deliver on all those change requests, and finish those current projects so you can start new ones (there will always be new ones). At risk of sounding like a psychedelic poster, this means accepting the things you can't change and changing the things you can.

What can't you change right now?

---

people (yecchh), followed by someone figuring out that the total cost of IT for the company went up, what with duplication and stovepipe systems mushrooming everywhere. So, most companies are back to a more centralized structure these days.

[2] One of my favourite quotes from Scott Adams is, "There is only one number 1 company in your industry, and chances are you are not working for them."

- The installed base of legacy systems.

- The backlog of change requests and bugs (even if you do manage to deal with a lot of these things, there will be new ones come along to take their place; that is job security).

- Senior management's' conflicting priorities for IT.

What can you change (or at least start to change?)

- The structuring and management of the IT projects.

- Overall management of staff by skills/specialties.

- Allocation of staff to the projects.

What follows in the rest of this book is my prescription for this change, supported by some war stories, lessons learned, and lots of ideas to try. Even an 'average' company has some unique aspects, so maybe not everything in this book will work for everyone, but I hope to give you enough ideas that some *will* work. My own fervent belief is that visible success with IT projects may lead to softening/improvement of the things you can't change right now.

And why should you believe me?

David Wright is a veteran of over 25 years in the IT trenches. He started as a programmer in the mainframe-dominated 80's, followed by 20 years as a Business Analyst and Architect, supplemented with stints in project management and testing when limited resources required it.

Mr. Wright has spent time both in operational areas delivering enhanced and new business systems, and in research and development focusing on information system methodologies and tools. The companies he has served in these capacities have ranged from life insurance to express delivery to equipment leasing & financing. In those companies, he has supported both the operational business and supporting functions like Finance, Human Resources, and even IT administration systems.

Sound good enough? If so, let's get started.

FORWARD – How will we document this? Start with Principles.

Like you, I have read my fair share of IT books, and each author has to decide how to best present what they are trying to communicate. One way is to describe the problems/opportunities of interest to the reader, then document the new approach or method that solves the problems; the reverse is to document the new approach/method first and then describe what problems it fixes.

I would like to try a mixture of the two, in the context of a set of Principles that I think will put all the content of this book in context. This is not an original idea, I must admit, as many manifestos and proclamations have been used to introduce new ways of things; the Agile Manifesto is well known (http://agilemanifesto.org/), and I am a particular fan of the Business Rules Manifesto (http://www.businessrulesgroup.org/brmanifesto.htm). These and others like them lay out the basic reasons for their existence and the value they provide.

Principles can be very effective; the best I have ever seen were created by Mao Tse-tung for the new Chinese Red Army after his first insurrection failed. His principals for protracted/attrition warfare was summed up in "a sixteen character military guide that even an illiterate peasant could understand...

> Enemy advances, we retreat.
> Enemy halts, we harass.
> Enemy tires, we attack.
> Enemy retreats, we pursue."[3]

Effective words, against which I hope my own do not completely whither in comparison.

---

[3] "Warrior Mao", MHQ magazine, Spring 2007, page 6.

So what are these new IT principles I propose?

1. *There is always more work to be done than people to do it.*

2. *Projects change the business, so know the overall business first.*

3. *Use an overall Architecture to describe the business, before and after projects.*

4. *Pick the right project(s) for the business.*

5. *Once a project is started, finish it.*

6. *Specialize – each member of a team assigned to a project should do what they do best for the length of that project.*

7. *One Architect/Analyst can generate enough work for two Developers and one Tester, structure your project teams in this ratio.*

8. *It's the Deliverable (that matters), not the Task.*

9. *Leave a record of what you have done, so the project will not miss you if you leave.*

10. *Models are better than text.*

11. *Partition large projects into 3 month phases, which is the longest period you can plan for without the chance of significant change to priorities, resources, etc.*

12. *Within the three month phase, parcel work into two-week periods; analyze for 2 weeks, then design and develop for 2 weeks (2 developers), and then test for 2 weeks. When the first 2 weeks of analysis is done, start the next two weeks of analysis in parallel to the design/development; carry on in cascading 2 week periods until the entire project scope has been addressed.*

13. *Given many medium to small software Deliverables, use architecture to manage and integrate the Deliverables into a complete system.*

I consider these a work in progress so, like most inventors of new principles or practices, I have come up with an overall name to encompass them, for now and as they evolve. It is:

Cascade – Better practices for effective delivery of information systems in a multi-project environment. ©

Let's look briefly at what each principle means or implies; which will serve as introductions to the remaining chapters that cover the principles in more detail.

1. *There is always more work to be done than people to do it.*

> Bordering on glibness, this principle summarizes the reality of virtually all organizations and activities, not just Information Systems delivery. It implies that a group within an organization charged with delivery of end results will a have a back-log of work not yet done. The existence of such a back-log is in itself not a problem, it reflects the desire of an organization to solve new problems and actively improve itself; the problem arises when it grows perceptively in size from management's perspective, and the length of time a change item sits on the back-log increases such that it can be measured in numbers of months or years.
>
> So, we must accept that there will be a backlog; fully eliminating it would mean that the delivery group (like IT) becomes redundant, or that the overall organization has stagnated. What must be done is to embrace the back-log; it is IT's input material and should be managed as such.

2.   *Projects change the business, so know the overall business first.*

A never-ending discussion in IT circles is about how much IT staff needs to know about the business that the information systems are supporting. It is high-lighted by every want-ad for an IT job that says previous experience in the employer's industry is mandatory.

Is detailed industry knowledge[4] and experience absolutely necessary for an IT job? No.

Can an IT staffer be effective with absolutely no knowledge of their employer's industry?   No.

As in many situations like this, the 'Yes' answer lies somewhere between the two extremes. Like a pendulum, the level of industry knowledge will vary across this spectrum, based on the specific organization, and by the particular IT role; e.g. Analysts need to know more than Programmers, and it justifiably argued that Testers need to know even more than Analysts.

So, some industry knowledge is required. I suggest from experience, however. that several week's research on an industry is equivalent to several year's work experience, as much of a person's experience is rendered out-of-date by industry changes, or is too specific to the company they worked at. This is truer today than ever, as the ubiquitous Web makes information about almost anything available with a text string and few mouse clicks.

As a result, IT needs to know something about the business going into a project, and the willingness to learn more as a project progresses.

---

[4] The IT term used in this context is *domain*, as in business domain knowledge.

The addendum to this discussion, however, is how much does IT need to know about the specific way their employer conducts business when competing in their industry[5]. Again from experience, I suggest that very little or no such knowledge is needed going into a project. The cliché that "a little knowledge is a dangerous thing" applies here. If IT people know too much about the current business, they may be unconsciously constrained when devising new IT solutions by 'the way things have always been done here.' In extreme cases, this can lead to an IT staffer having the delusional belief that they know more about the business than the systems users and their management.

Do not fall victim to this belief. IT is about underlying hardware and infrastructure, and the information systems that run on them. The systems' users and their management --- supported by all the strategies, policies, procedures and rules that define and control the business --- will know the specifics of their business better than IT; their jobs depend on it.

This is not to imply that all business users & management are omniscient, or that all businesses operate without duplications or errors, or that there are not things the business doesn't know yet. In fact, effective use of IT can address many such issues in the operation of a business, but IT and IT people do this in support of the business; IT does not define the business.

So, know your business in order to support your business.

3.   *Use Architecture to describe the business, before and after projects.*

"Architecture" is becoming a more widely used term associated with Information Technology. The number of adjectives applied to the term seems endless: "Technical

---

[5] This Principle also applies to non-profit organizations, government, etc.; the measures of success are different than in private sector industries, but the role(s) of IT are essentially the same.

Architecture", "Systems Architecture", "Business Systems Architecture", "Enterprise Architecture", and so on, so it must be important.

Why do we need Architecture?

Architecture is not an end in itself; Architecture exists because things need to be built.

Architecture is required when building anything that is not simple; in its essence, Architecture identifies all the separate components of an end product and how all the components are related and fit together to comprise the whole of the product.

Architecture is layered to capture and present information about the product to different audiences, from initial/high concept to detailed specification.

Applied to IT, a component assembly approach is dominating the industry, from the OO approach of software development, to real-time use of defined services, as popularized by SOA. Specialized agent software is starting to assist in finding services and brokering between different services to perform transactions collaboratively.

For the average company using IT, architecture is needed because it needs focused IT functionality to deliver the highest current value, while trying hard to ensure that the function will work ("integrate") with the next function that is needed.

It should be emphasized that this is Architecture for Information Systems.; there are methods and approaches being promoted for an overall "Business Architecture", architecture for the whole business, not just IT. Originating from IT circles, they often look like an IT/IS architecture, which can be confusing. The Architecture in this book is definitely about Information Technology and Systems.

What is an Information System?

Computers are used for many different purposes, often with very specialized hardware and software; examples range from missile guidance systems, to supercomputers crunching numbers for scientists at high speeds. On the other hand, personal computers and the internet that use common hardware and software platforms have become a part of daily personal life, whether to play more and more sophisticated video games, or to write blogs, among other things.

However, if you use a computer as a regular part of your workday, you are likely not doing any of the things mentioned in the previous paragraph. Instead, you are probably using a computer to do business as part of your job in the private or public sectors; you might also be self-employed or otherwise own your own business, but in any case, I know you are not playing Half-Life 2... You are most definitely using an "Information System".

The good news is that you do not need to invent an IT Architecture method for your company. Many authors and vendors have methods available already. When starting out, I recommend investigating/adopting the architecture that started it all, the "Zachman Framework" as developed and enhanced by John Zachman. He devised a matrix framework that cross-references core information concepts against the levels of abstraction that are used by different audiences and participants in delivery of Information Systems.

The key benefit of the framework is that it illustrates how information concepts can be transformed through the levels to produce operating components of the needed Information Systems.

Levels of Abstraction / Viewpoints: (www.zifa.com)

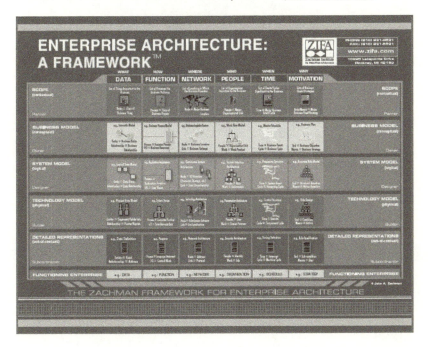

Last two points on Zachman:

- The cross points of the Concept columns and Abstraction rows are called "Cells"; each cell will group the methods or documents (artifacts) that describe the content of the cell. Zachman does not specify what artifacts to use, or what methodologies to use to create the artifacts. The things in each cell on the diagram are just suggestions. Keep this in mind for Principle #10.

- The Framework looks two-dimensional, but it is actually multi-dimensional when artifacts in one cell are cross-referenced to artifacts in other cells, the most obvious example is What vs. How, i.e., what function creates specific occurrences of data.

17

Again, from www.zifa.com

4. Pick the right project(s) for the business.

At any one time, the IT department of an average company is running multiple projects. How did they get started? How were they even defined as a project that needed to be carried out?

No one may actually know. In more chaotic environments, projects can start as a seed of an idea, pick up momentum and resources if a manager or two can see that they will benefit from the project. At some point, the project will bump into another one, usually because they both want the same IT staff or other resources. Strong managers can often come out of these resource conflicts with what they need for their project, while the other managers suffer from their project going on hold or being cancelled. Otherwise, the conflict is escalated until one common, higher manager has to step in and decide who gets what; and this is often the first time the higher manager has even heard about the projects.

I sat in on a senior management committee meeting where the progress to date of a grand project was presented and a request for a budget increase was made to complete the project. The CEO took all this in, and commented that this was very interesting, but given the sizable amounts of money and time expended so far, why the heck had he never heard of this project before? The next week my manager sent me to see the CIO, who charged me with coming up with a new process for defining, approving, and controlling IT projects, better known these days as 'Project Governance'.

So, how do you pick the 'right' IT projects? First you have to make the choice explicit, avoiding the random start-ups described above; do encourage any and everyone to suggest possible projects. An active strategic and operational planning process will also tend to drive out new projects as senior and middle management look for IT assistance to reach their assigned goals. All these proposed project ideas then become input to a 'gating' process, supported by means of valuing the worth of a project like, but not limited to, cost-benefit analyses.

5.   *Once a project is started, finish it.*

Even with a good process to pick the right projects to execute, there will be a strong if unrecognized tendency to initiate too many projects at once, or initiate more projects before any already underway have been completed. This goes back to the average senior manager's split view that most IT spending is a waste, except for their own projects. Given several senior managers in an organization expressing these views, a natural reaction is to have at least one project underway for each manager; if most of the IT efforts are applied to projects for only a few managers, the rest will complain or start looking for other options.

However, trying to run too many projects at once ends up pleasing no one, as no project makes any noticeable enough progress to be seen as a success, so the result is that no one is happy with IT's performance, even IT.

So, projects have to be run such that at least one is completing within each reporting period; this would be quarterly in most companies. In large IT shops with dozens of projects, it may be a percentage you aim for, 10% to 20% of projects completed per period. Given the common situation of limited IT resources, allocating these resources to a set of projects has to be guided by a focus on completion, not competing priorities.

6.   *Specialize – each member of a team assigned to a project should do what they do best for the length of that project.*

This principle supports #5 above. With limited resources, there is another strong tendency to have IT staff 'wear multiple hats' on a project, especially the Business Analyst who is asked to also be the Project Manager and/or Lead Tester. Rather than getting more than you are paying for, you get less as an IT Staffer skilled in one role spends more time performing the other roles than an appropriate specialist would, and is distracted from being productive in their primary role.

At any time, and perhaps more so currently, there will be debates about which is better, a generalist or a specialist. I will agree that a strong, experienced generalist who can cover a wide number of tasks is the best resource you can have. However, these people are rare, and the odds of having even one such person in your average IT department are low[6]. So, make sure that your staff is doing what they do best as much as possible as often as possible.

---

[6] The popular concept since the arrival of the Agile Manifesto is that of the 'Generalizing Specialist'. Ignoring the oxymoronic nature of the phrase, proponents of Agile Approaches do say these types of people are (1) necessary for Agile to work, and (2) are hard to find and keep. They recommend that you do not try being

(This is not to say that people may not learn new roles over time, either switching to different roles or aspiring to be that coveted generalist. However, this is the task of overall resource management, overhead which will take up some portion of a person's productive time. This is why most project management methods usually assume only about 6 out of each 8 hours can be used on actual projects. This reduced availability speaks even more to the value of specialization at a point in time. It also speaks to the value of matrix management, where Project Managers manage the projects and Resource Managers handle the 'care and feeding' of the valuable IT staff assigned to projects.)

7. One Architect/Analyst can generate enough work for two Developers and one Tester, structure your project teams in this ratio.

This is actually one of those "rules of thumb" that have been borne out over time. (The ratio may vary a bit from case to case, like when the experience levels are different across the roles.) This ratio combines with the specialization of principle #6 to form the strong basis for the Cascade effect covered in the later principles.

I will be using the most common 'role titles' of analyst, designer, developer, and tester for the remainder of this book. Sometimes these roles have different names, and there are many other roles in IT overall, but these four are the most recognizable to anyone doing primarily project work. (And the Project Manager makes five! Can't forget them...)

'Agile' without such people, i.e. everyone else should not try this; but 'everyone else' is who makes up the bulk of your IT department, so you must make the most effective use of all your people to be successful.

8. It's the Deliverable (that matters), not the Task.

The final deliverable is the Information System ready to be used effectively by the Business. If you can jump from 'Start' to this final deliverable in one "Task", then power to you. Some people can do this; most cannot. This is again where a team of specialists is most effective on an average project.

This means that the project work will be divided into many tasks, sub-tasks, etc. . . . Once assigned a task, it is the goal of a specialist to produce a deliverable/result/artifact that can be used by the next specialist to further the progress of the overall project. Unfortunately, this simple idea has been the starting point for literally hundreds of IS delivery methodologies, many which spend an inordinate amount of content explaining how to do a task, how to amass all the tasks in Phases, and often insisting that its way is mandatory for success.

What this can lead to is an over-emphasis on the how of IT project tasks, to the detriment of actually completing them with all due speed. Here we see the task that is 90% done for weeks, or the infamous 'analysis paralysis' where a project cannot seem to get past Requirements. Ends do not justify any means, but Ends must be delivered.

9. Leave a record of what you have done, so the project will not miss you if you leave.

If change is the only constant, then resources on a project will change. The risk in such change is that a person's contribution to a project will be lost, and that the new person assigned to the project will have to start over. This is a particular risk in "quick and dirty" projects where an operating result is produced, but no one else can understand the code that was produced. However, if the contribution involves producing quality artifacts as described in #8 above, there is always a point-in-time record of what has been accomplished so far, which can be used by new project resources to continue the project with minimal disruption.

10. *Models are better than text.*

I would like to think that by this point in time, this principle no longer requires justification. It has been at least a few years since I last saw a dense "SRD" or "SDD" document (SYSTEM REQUIREMENTS DOCUMENT, SYSTEM DESIGN DOCUMENT). I must offer my respect to the many talented people who labored to produce these documents over the decades; these documents were at least a step up from no Requirements or Design artifacts at all.

Consider what a 'model' really is in general; it is a representation of a finished product in a scaled down version; engineers have been literally creating models of what they are going to build for centuries, for such reasons as testing out problems on a small scale, and for presenting a view of the end result to whomever may be paying for it.

At this point, though, let us abandon any other aspect of *physical* engineering as an analogy for Information Systems development. Software is different; while tools and bridges and buildings have been created to either extend or protect the physical capabilities of human beings, Information Systems are created to extend the our mental capabilities, to help our thinking.

Given that, software can still be engineered, but it is a different type of Engineering. Software or Information Engineering has existed as a known concept since the 1970's, although anyone who thought to call themselves a software engineer usually incurred the wrath, or at least disdain, of the established Engineering Disciplines and Schools. I am not an engineer, would not claim to be one, but my understanding is that traditional engineering is addressing software within its disciplines. In the future, as software becomes even more critical to our well-being and safety, it may be that those who design and create software will have to be accredited engineers, just like the ones who design and build bridges. I think history shows that quite a few early bridges and other structures were prone to collapse before engineering principles started to prevent it. Software is only a half-century old, so even in the age of internet speed and high change, more time will be needed to bring software in line with other long time products.

In the meantime, it should be a goal for all of us in the IT business to adopt useful aspects of engineering to improve the quality of software, and modeling is a key concept to adopt. It almost frightens me that many still promote programming as an art form, that code can be beautiful or exquisite in some way. Well, even the most obscure art needs an audience to appreciate it, and it can't just be other artists. Software is a product to be used, not admired, so if anything, programmers of the past 50 years have been more like craftsmen, using individual skills and experience to produce useful 'objects' for society to use. The problem is that demand continues to out-strip programmer output (remember the backlog!), so improved, repeatable and transferable methods are needed to transform software development from a craft to a true industry.

11.   *Partition large projects into 3 month phases, that is the longest period you can plan for without the chance of significant change to priorities, resources, etc.*

I was lucky to learn this early in the 90's as Project Management was getting a higher profile, accompanied by the increased use of Microsoft Project. Other PM tools were in use, but usually in limited numbers; MS Project, on the other hand, was readily available and budding Project Managers thought they could now plan the whole world for months or years in advance. What actually happened, however, was constant re-planning as the reality of business change and resource turnover always took their toll. As Napoleon said, "A plan is only good until the battle is joined."

After that, one must adapt to the changes that will always come.

My own experience was on a large project that was broken into a dozen pieces, which were planned separately to a target 18 months away, at which point I was asked to integrate them into one plan while resolving resource conflicts. First thing, we found was that MS Project of that time crashed when you reached around a thousand tasks.

So, it was about this time that some IBM PM consultants were brought on to sort out this mess, and where I first heard the above principle. Yes, you need a plan to get started and to control a project over time. You can even sketch out a plan out over many months to see and communicate the big picture; but, do not commit to any target date over 3 months away; odds are you will miss it. This also means you should do the detailed planning only to the next target date, meaning the full WBS and resource assignment. (At the other end of the detail level, the IBM consultants also recommended that the shortest task in your WBS should be 2 weeks, no less, otherwise you are micro-managing.)

Once you have a detailed plan for three months, and a high-level plan for the rest of the project, you can add more detail to further target dates as the project progresses, as each interim target is reached or on a rolling month-by-month basis. The level of change in any 3 month period will be manageable, much more than over the whole project.

There is a more recent corollary to the three month principle; the age of the mega-project should be over by now. Any IS project that takes many months or years to deliver the system is destined to fail. Yes, large systems are still needed, but break them into pieces that can be delivered, ideally about every 3 months; longer than that and you start to slide back to the mega-project approach, while shorter than that will not produce enough of the system to be worth delivering to the business. All business works in 3 month quarter cycles anyway, IT should too.

12. Within the three month phase, parcel work into two-week periods; analyze for 2 weeks, then design and develop for 2 weeks (two developers), and then test for 2 weeks. When the first 2 weeks of analysis is done, start the next two weeks of analysis in parallel to the design/development; carry on in cascading 2 week periods until the entire project scope has been addressed.

OK, a 64 word-long paragraph is pushing the boundary of a 'Principle', but this point is the basic building block of Cascade. Are two week periods too aggressive? I think not, based on experience. I find developers and a tester like to work in such quick bursts, as delivering more results faster makes anyone feel more productive and accomplished, and illustrate quickly what works and doesn't work. However, small bits delivered quickly need to be integrated into an overall solution, which leads to Principle #13.

13. Given many medium to small software Deliverables, use Architecture to manage and integrate the Deliverables into a complete system.

This is a more specific statement of Principle #3; in Cascade, an Information System Architecture is used to integrate the two week deliverables, until a complete deliverable (component, sub-system) is assembled.

In parallel, a release schedule is a great approach to support delivery. Gather the usable deliverables into timed releases that go into production together. As per Principle #11, a Release each quarter is recommended. The business receives what they are paying for often enough to be of value, but not often enough such that assimilation of change is so frequent it causes chaos.

The rest of this book is organized in chapters, of course, more or less around the Principles, *but structured independently so you can start with what interests you most and then move in the order than works for you, the reader.*

CHAPTER ONE – There is always more work to be done than people to do it.

Current Projects

A number of current projects (are) being carried out, that no one can remember when they started and, even if some target date has been set, no reasonable expectation exists that they will end soon. … Each person (working on projects) is probably assigned to multiple of those current projects, juggling the work and trying to determine what they should really be working on.

This is the low-hanging fruit of the average IT department. The absolute first priority is to wind-up as many of these projects as possible, as soon as possible. This sounds like common-sense; it is certainly sensible, but not at all common.

No rocket-science here, you need to allocate all your resources to a subset of the on-going projects, get some successful project deliveries, and then look around for new opportunities. If you have a large slate of current projects, you may need to do this again (and again) for another subset of projects. Keep doing this until the number of current projects no longer exceeds your capacity to resource them, or as close as you can get. Do your utmost to avoid initiating any new projects while cleaning up the current projects.[7]

It also helps if you can manage to identify any existing projects that can be cancelled out-right. This will not be totally in your control, as the business unit or sponsor that wants the project done may resist. It is just to your advantage to identify any projects that are clearly no longer needed, and for which the sunk costs should be capped.

---

[7] Of course, some projects cannot be delayed; especially changes needed for new legislation or other compliance issues. Jump on those immediately and get them done quickly so you can get back to the other on-going projects.

How many projects should you focus on as described above? You can't overload a project either, without incurring diminishing returns. A rule-of-thumb would be to define the number of people on a typical project team in your shop, and then divide that number into the total number of people you have available for projects. There are many ideas and opinions about optimum team size, usually around 7 plus or minus 2.

Which subset of projects should be focused on first? If no other factors are in play, choose the projects that most closely look to be near completion. This can be difficult, given the "90% done" syndrome[8]; you may focus on a 90% done project and find it is more like only 10% done in reality(!), at which point I would drop it and move on to a more promising project.

Other factors can be applied in selecting projects sub-set; they depend a lot on how much information you have on your projects, and can include:

- *Expected Business Value or Return On Investment*: If you already have some notion of the value of a delivering a project, especially a cost-benefit analysis, you can try attacking the projects with the highest value *if that is something your business management will appreciate.* Many companies are good at defining value or benefit up-front, but only the better companies take the time after a project is complete to confirm if the benefits really were realized. If your company does not do this yet, suggest they start, but avoid this factor for selecting the projects subset until they do start.

- *Project Priority*, which can be determined based on a combination of Business Value and/or other Project Drivers. This is often a weighted calculation where values are assigned based on how well a project addresses items such as 'increased sales', 'improved decision-making', 'better customer service', etc. . Each project has a priority value to

---

[8] …where tasks on a project are quickly reported as being 50% done, 75% done, 90% done… then they stall, with the last 10% appearing difficult or impossible to complete.

compare to others, and highest-priority projects are initiated first.

If you have a Priority value assigned for your projects, but it really hasn't been the key factor in initiating projects, then start using it; that's pretty obvious, I know. What is more likely is that priority did play a part in initiating projects, but has not carried over to decisions made during projects. If your projects are now executing out-of-priority order, see if re-ordering them will help in faster delivery and increased business value.

- *When all else fails, Ask. (Or just start with Ask.).* It will be no big secret if you have many projects underway with no ends in sight. It is also likely that many current stakeholders may not have been involved when some of the projects were started. So, you can meet with these stakeholders to determine what their current priorities are and which projects are of most value to them.

  The usual issue with this approach is: who should I ask? In a perfect situation, I look for the person highest in the organization whose span of control covers all departments who sponsored or are impacted by the projects.
  However, this person could be senior enough in the company that they may decline to help you, preferring to delegate to his reports.

  Querying and meeting with this group may give you the priorities you need; or, it may illustrate any politics or power struggles that are on-going, for which you may be able to facilitate a resolution or at least a compromise...or not. In the latter case, it may be necessary to escalate this back to groups' common manager for resolution.

So, one or more of the above factors may assist you in identifying the best sub-set of projects to first target for quick completion. If no strong values or priorities can be discerned, I would default to those that can finish the fastest.

The Backlog

Along with a set of current projects, your IT department will also have collected a large back-log of requested changes to the installed base of systems, overlaid with a long list of problems/bugs in the systems that the business is currently 'working around' until they ever get fixed. This may or may not also include requests for brand new systems at your company, but I include all of these as part of the overall backlog.

The logical sequence is to address the backlog once the current projects are under control, but neither should it be ignored up front. When you have picked the projects to be completed first, you should also review the backlog for any items that could be added to a current project, without unduly increasing the cost or elapsed time of the project.

A core of change requests will remain, of course. They will vary in scope and impact from a one-liner request to add a new field to a system, to a formal proposal to significantly improve an existing system and/or deliver new functionality/systems. Your backlog list may be quite large, but here I reiterate that this is not something to be feared; a back-log is the primary source of new work for an IT department.

Any large list needs to be organized into groupings by similar properties to make them easier to address in projects. Proposals for new systems as mentioned above will normally remain as separate efforts, spawning their own independent projects. This leaves a list of small to medium change requests.

One common way to group the requests is by the current system they are requesting changes for. Most change request processes I have seen usually tag requests by system when they are first received and logged. Other properties that can be used include: name and department of requestor, date requested, priority requested, etc.

If you have a lot of requests for any one system, a maintenance project for the system should be considered. If requests for the system have come in on a regular basis and will continue to do so, you may want to adopt a scheduled maintenance release approach, where projects of about 3 months in length are carried out in sequence over time, each release adding more to the system in a planned process to minimize the impact of change on end-users. Of course, maintenance projects can be defined and carried out on an as-needed basis as well.

Just remember not to initiate new maintenance projects while still trying to get current projects under control. Once control is achieved, maintenance projects can be considered for initiation.

Results

Moving from an uncontrolled project environment to a controlled environment, even slowly but steadily, will reap benefits for the Business, IT Management and the IT Staff who do the work. Finishing projects that provide business value is the key to long term IT success. IT Staff that know what they are working on is valuable, and see its value realized, frankly like their jobs more; tie everyone's bonus remuneration to enterprise success that depends on IT delivery, and that is the proverbial cherry on the cake.

CHAPTER TWO – Projects change the business, so know the overall business first.

The core of any enterprise, profit or non-profit, is the differentiated goods and/or services it delivers to paying customers.[9] Essential to an enterprise's success is the resources it marshals and the processes that employ those resources to produce goods and services. The approaches to organizing those resources and managing those processes are multitudinous and varied, but one common division across average enterprises is that between operations and support (or line and staff).

No goods and services producing process exist in isolation. Not far removed are product/service development and marketing, to ensure the enterprise is producing the things its customers want. Farther removed are supporting functions like Human Resources, Accounting and, yes, IT. Most companies have some lawyers working in a legal department, but that does not make those companies into law firms. Accounting is a very standardized function, with some industry variations (like liability reporting in insurance), but an accountant can move between companies and industries and still be effective. This is also true of most IT roles, and we should all recognize that is the case.

So, at an average company, IT is part of the support for the core business, just like Accountants and Lawyers and HR Administrators and such. It is possible that a very skilled and intelligent support person can know as much about the business as operations staff doing the work, but that is a rare person. Otherwise, good support people should concentrate on being the best they can in their roles, to be part of overall enterprise team delivering those goods and services.

---

[9] A quick aside: don't buy into this crap that IT is a business within a business serving internal customers; there are no internal customers. Customers are external parties who choose to pay for something the enterprise provides; everyone working within that enterprise is part of a team that should be working together to satisfy customers and remain in business.

Still, the debate about how much IT staff needs to know about the business rages on. As was mentioned in the Forward, it is highlighted by every want-ad for an IT job that says previous experience in the employer's industry is mandatory. I will reiterate that detailed industry knowledge and experience is not necessary for IT Staff to be an effective contributor, but neither is ignorance bliss.

How much <u>do</u> you need to know, then? You need to learn enough about how information is used by the business to be able identify and deliver information systems that will improve and increase the business' capabilities to deliver its outputs. That's a wide-ranging answer, because everyone starts with a unique level of knowledge, including sometimes starting with none at all.

I started my career in life and health insurance and was in that industry for a long time. As an entry-level person in my first IT job, I believe I was hired partly because of my Computer Science degree, but also because I exhibited willingness and some ability to learn. I actually spent a decade in this industry before ever working on an insurance system; the domains I was involved in included mortgage investments, stocks and bonds, investment reporting, some accounting, and even systems for IT, using system usage logs to allocate computing costs to business divisions. Each time I switched domains, I usually started with little knowledge, like only knowing how a mortgage worked because I had one (!). Given such a minimal start, I would read a lot of material about the domain, at both an industry level and documentation specific to the company. This approach also worked when I left insurance to work in express delivery, and more recently in large equipment leasing and finance.

Yes, there was at least one time where a business department manager complained that it took too long for IT to learn about his operations, but that was an exception. Over time I have found that a willingness to learn combined with admitting that you don't know everything yet has been received well by the vast majority of business people I have worked with over nearly 30 years.

However, most companies' still desire to hire IT people with previous domain experience. Granted, starting with more than zero knowledge can get things going faster and sooner, but that advantage is relatively small when factored over large or multiple projects. In fact, as mentioned in the forward, IT people who let their previous experience influence current work may actually constrain or limit the solutions they recommend to the business.

And yes, what must be avoided is the belief that you know as much or more than operations people and only you know what is best for the business. I have seen that sense of superiority rewarded with an escort to the door.

So, IT at an average company is and will continue to be a support function for the foreseeable future, and should focus on being part of the overall enterprise team. If that's not for you, head to a software company.

CHAPTER THREE – Use architecture to describe the business, before and after projects.

As of this writing, Architecture seems to be on the upswing as a recognized aspect of effective information systems delivery and use. The most common term is, again, "Enterprise", as in "Enterprise Architecture".

My own first exposure to Architecture dates back (way back) to about 1988, when I first learned about Information Engineering, as in the Information Engineering Methodology (IEM) then offered by James Martin & Associates.

From http://en.wikipedia.org/wiki/Information_Engineering

> *Information Engineering (IE) or Information Engineering Methodology (IEM) is an approach to designing and developing information systems. It has a somewhat chequered history that follows two very distinct threads. It is said to have originated in Australia between 1976 and 1980, and appears first in the literature in 1981 in the Savant Institute publication 'Information Engineering' by James Martin and Clive Finkelstein.*

By 1988, I had shifted roles from my start as a programmer into analysis, also expanding my knowledge of the emerging System Development Life Cycle (SDLC). A lot of companies, including my own, had attempted to define their own standard SDLC, and the word "methodology" seemed to be on everyone's lips. Consulting companies came out of the wood-work, plying their own methodologies with sales pitches of great success if you bought the product and some consulting hours too.

Many of these were based on the earlier methods of structured analysis and design (developed by Ken Orr, Larry Constantine, Vaughn Frick, Ed Yourdon, Steven Ward and others) and the favourite artifact of the time, the Data Flow Diagram (DFD). In

35

parallel, the data model (as developed by Peter Chen, Thomas Bachman and others) began to emerge in a pairing with relational methods of E. F. Codd.

During this time I used a few such methods on some projects, along with early tools like Excelerator (we got a boxed version 1.0 which the salesman got out of the trunk of his car in front of our office after driving to Toronto from Boston!). These were ad-hoc uses of methods and tools while the in-house developed methodology withered away.

My experience on these projects led, to my great good luck, to driving a new project to acquire a brand new methodology for the whole company. This is when my research into the state of the art in commercial methodologies introduced me to Information Engineering, and it introduced me to Architecture in Information Systems. James Martin had recently published his trilogy of Information Engineering books, and was emerging as the new guru of information systems.

The core of Information Engineering was its 3 layers of Architecture. First, Data and Function models made up the Information Architecture, describing the key concepts/entities of the business for which data was collected, and the functions that managed that data to be valid and useable. The catch-phrase was "Data + Function = Information".

Next, analytical techniques like affinity analysis were used to partition the Information Architecture into distinct Business Areas, cohesive groupings of data and function that could be developed separately and then later integrated into a whole systems environment for the enterprise; this was the Business Systems Architecture. Further analysis of the operational needs of the Business Systems led to the definition of the Technical Architecture, detailing the physical environment needed to implement the business systems. This was the use of Architecture in the full sense of what I described in the Forward.

These architectures were not an end in themselves; they each played a role in leading to delivery of an integrated set of information systems meeting the needs of the business. The scope of these architectures was an enterprise, not one product or project. They showed that the systems of an enterprise supported different business areas, such that highly cohesive and de-coupled systems could be built, almost in parallel, and they would all work together as portfolio of systems to support the information needs of the enterprise.

The architecture(s) of Information Engineering were a great discovery for me, but it became clear over time that they assumed, especially as automated by CASE tools, that other aspects of Systems would be handled outside their scope, such as user roles/security, or locations/networks.

In the same period of time, however, John Zachman was developing his own ideas on what architecture could do for information systems, as described in the Forward.

Who is John Zachman? (from www.zifa.com)

> *John A. Zachman is the originator of the "Framework for Enterprise Architecture" which has received broad acceptance around the world as an integrative framework, or "periodic table" of descriptive representations for Enterprises. Mr. Zachman is not only known for this work on Enterprise Architecture, but is also known for his early contributions to IBM's Information Strategy methodology (Business Systems Planning) as well as to their Executive team planning techniques (Intensive Planning).*

> *Mr. Zachman retired from IBM in 1990, having served them for 26 years. He is Chief Executive Officer of the Zachman Institute for Framework Advancement (ZIFA), an organization dedicated to advancing the conceptual and implementation states of the art in Enterprise Architecture. He presently is Chairman of the Board of Zachman Framework Associates, a worldwide consortium managing*

conformance to the Zachman Framework principles. He also operates his own education and consulting business, Zachman International.

So, how should we describe the Business in Architecture? No surprise, models will be your primary means. Within the concept of Architecture, we should remember that Finklestein and Martin called their approach Information *Engineering*. The concepts they adopted from overall engineering disciplines were the value of modeling a thing before you build it, including the ability to test/validate a model before using it as input to building the actual product.

That is all well and fine, but what does a business model look like? Information Systems development is still a young discipline, so no one modeling format or standard has become the standard. Its relative youth also lead to some concerns from traditional engineering disciplines, that IS approaches were still way too immature and un-disciplined to merit being called 'Engineering'. I think this concern is lessened over time, as many engineering schools now include software engineering programs, but I don't believe even different academic programs agree on just what software engineering is yet.

That leaves us with the need to define or adopt some modeling methods to use in describing the information needs of the enterprise; there are certainly many available to choose from, and author David C. Hay has done every one a great favour in collecting them in his book "Requirements Analysis: *From Business Views to Architecture*". What I can do here is discuss models I have used and my experiences. Given the influence of Zachman, I now start with the simple lists of Row 1 to provide context and scope:

- List of Things of Interest to the Business
- List of Processes the Business Performs
- List of Locations in Which The Business Operates
- List of Organizations of Importance to the Business
- List of Events/Cycle of Significance to the Business
- List of Business Goals/Strategies

List of Things of Interest to the Business

Given the shared goal of most companies to profitably (or effectively for a non-profit) supply a product or service, a lot of things will be common, such as:

- Customers
- Suppliers
- Product
- Service
- Employees
- Etc.

These will break-down into many entities in row 2.

List of Processes the Business Performs

These could include:

- Acquire Customers
- Acquire resources
- Manufacture Product
- Perform Service
- Sell Product
- Etc.

List of Locations in Which the Business Operates

This is something that is overlooked these days, because networks make it easy to do business anywhere; that is an amazing accomplishment given to us by Network Engineers, whose work the rest us of don't really understand.

On the other hand, business process and rules may vary from country to country, due to different laws, and these should be captured by jurisdiction/location.

List of Organizations of Importance to the Business

All people belong to one organization or another, either formal (marketing department) or informal (attendees at a baseball game), for long or short periods of time; from an IT perspective, we are looking at groups and individuals who will use or be impacted by an information system.

List of Events/Cycle of Significance to the Business

Time waits for no Enterprise, and no Enterprise is independent of time. Here you want to list the external events (at least) that initiate activity in the enterprise, like "Customer places Order"; internal events may also be of significance at this level, like "Stock inventory has dropped below required level."

Cycles are those aspects of your business where things of importance begin in one state and 'flow' though intermediate states to a final state, like Order Received, Order Approved, Ordered Packaged, Order Shipped, and so on. There are also calendar based cycles that can also spawn events, like "It is Time to produce Quarterly Financial Statements".

List of Business Goals/Strategies

This aspect of an enterprise has only recently started to play a specific role in information systems. Zachman's Motivation columns left many scratching their heads for a long time, mine included. Besides, we had enough to keep us busy in the rest of the columns.

However, we know now that it is this column that provides the guidance to everything that we know or do in the other columns. Every typical company is trying to be profitable, but each must have its own way to differentiate itself from its competition, so Goals and Strategies must be set. This statement is almost a no-brainer, as every company has mission statements, 5 Year Plans, Goals and Measures; the problem has been how to apply those in every day activities and the systems that support them. The answer today is

Business Rules, drawn from policies and procedures created to meet those goals; this is jumping ahead a bit, but this can be the column that gets ignored early on to the detriment of the enterprise's systems, so don't let that happen.

So, do all these lists count as models? Maybe not, but they drive the creation of models. Even at this high-level, some models can help to communicate scope to people who want a system, my favourite being the Context Diagram.

BUSINESS CONTEXT DIAGRAM SAMPLE

Source: Craig Borysowich[10]

Context is defined as "The circumstances in which an event occurs; a setting." (American Heritage Dictionary). "Event" stands out as the main artifact of our 'When' architecture question. So, we end up with a diagram that shows:

1) The events that an enterprise recognizes and responds to, either as they occur or are anticipated.
2) The processes that are initiated by an event occurrences, usually one event kicking of one end-to-end process, or a series of processes (parallel, asynchronous) that provides the desired response

---

[10] http://blogs.ittoolbox.com/eai/implementation/archives/context-diagrams-at-the-enterprise-level-14345

3) The external Parties that generate events and receive the enterprise's response.

This kind of diagram is already showing how items on the above Scope-level lists can be related to each other. This is already beginning to define what your Enterprise is, and knowing that will make it easier to run, and to change as needed.

Other high-level 'models' are algebraic-style matrices, where columns of one item are matched to rows of another item. Typical matrices include:

- Things of Interest *maintained by* Process
- Process *is carried out in* Location
- Organization/Person *performs* Process
- Event *initiates* Process (as described above)
- Policy *guides/constrains execution of* Process.

Given this scope-level architecture, you do need to move to a level of detail within that scope that describes the business in enough detail to make business and project decisions, which is Row 2 in the Zachman Framework. My own experience lies mainly in modeling of the first two columns, Data and Process

Data Model

'Things of Interest' to a business means a business wants to remember what it knows about those things, and capture what it discovers about new things. In a business architecture, this means defining what data about things that the business needs to capture and use, leading to definitions of files and databases in the subsequent Business Systems Architecture.

The most common format used to capture data requirements is the Entity-Relationship Diagram, which like Architecture, was most popularized by the Information Engineering Methodology. The main component is the Data Entity, a subject of interest to the Business, associated by the business relationships between them. Each entity contains data items/attributes that relate to or describe the Entity. Each attribute belongs only to one Entity, so duplication of data is reduced.

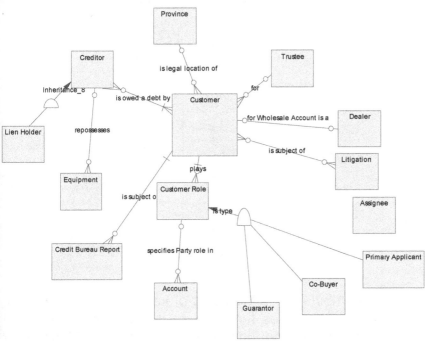

Sample Data Model

Functions / Processes

The functions/processes a business performs can be described in multiple ways in Architecture. Even the meaning of the words 'function' and 'process' can vary depending on the model one uses.

When defining a Business Architecture these days, I see 'Process' as defined in the Business Process (Re)Engineering discipline: a set of steps carried out in response to an event or trigger, producing the desired result. The structure of the Process is normally captured in a Map diagram, which can get very complicated quickly. They may not be very stable either, as processes are changed/improved all the time. The meat of a Process is in its constituent steps, where

43

Cascade

some amount of work is done and completed before the process moves on, such as "Create Customer Record" or "Print Late Notice". These are the basic information functions in the architecture, and note how they are all verb/noun phrases where the noun will be an entity or attribute in your data model.

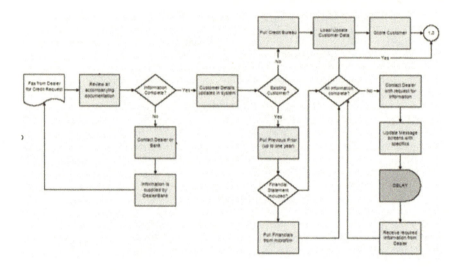

This verb/noun combination is the basis of key architecture artifact, the CRUD matrix. It matches functions to the data they use, and specifically as to whether the function Creates, Reads, Updates or Deletes the data.

	Customer	Customer Order	Customer Account	Customer Invoice	Vendor Invoice	Product
Maintain Customer Order	U		U		RU	
Terminate Customer Order	U		U		RU	
Receive Customer Order	R	C	CR			
Process Customer Order	CRU		RU			R
Fill Customer Order	RU		RU			RU
Invoice Customer	RU		RU	C		
Ship Customer Order			U		C	
Validate Vendor Invoice					R	
Pay Vendor Invoice					RU	
Maintain Inventory						CRUD

Source: Craig Borysowich[11]

The above models and their cross-reference in the CRUD are core to defining the architecture within which Information Systems are created, and therefore for defining the business and the impact IT projects will have. Expanding into the other columns of the Zachman Framework (a subject large enough for its own book and some have already been written) only increases the level of understanding of a business. As Rudyard Kipling wrote:

> I keep six honest serving-men (They taught me all I knew); Their names are What and Why and When And How and Where and Who."

CHAPTER FOUR– Pick the Right Projects for the Business

IT Projects have rightly earned the reputation over the years as places where lots of money goes in and no value comes out. We are all aware of the CHAOS[12] studies by the Standish Group that show most IT projects are also usually late, and a large number are never even completed(!).

How did this happen? My theory is that computers were first used to automate rote manual tasks, and the results from these projects were valuable and easily seen as so. This led to the belief that automating most anything was going to be good for the enterprise but, as projects moved into more complicated/complex aspects of the business, the returns of pure automation began to diminish. Unfortunately, it was still assumed that the value was there, and it was a complete assumption; actually determining what the value would be was done only rarely.

Early computer projects were run in the realm of the IT department, likely better known then as the Data Processing department. Business departments had been happy to get their worst drudge work automated, but the techie geek image of IT started at this time as well; so, the business would deal with IT as little as possible to get what they wanted, but otherwise considered IT as being on another planet. In this environment, one idea about using computers could snowball into a big project if enough people liked it.

So, projects proceeded into more complicated areas of the business, and they started to break down, some failed, and now Management wanted to know why, and also started asking if all these computer projects were worth what they cost (because costs were not assumed, they were measurable); and how did they all get started anyway?

---

[12] © The Standish Group 1995.

Chapter One has already described the most common result of this 'evolution', a lot of current projects *being carried out, that no one can remember when they started and, even if some target date has been set, no reasonable expectation exists that they will end soon.* Following the approaches suggested in Chapter One should get you to the point where the current projects are delivering and finishing, such that you and the business actually have the option of choosing a new project to begin, along with the awareness that such choices should be made in a way that avoids a return to the original mess.

That awareness should include:

1) A recognition that IT projects do not belong to IT, they belong to the Enterprise as a whole, even if various non-IT parts of the Enterprise are assigned responsibility for some sub-set of projects.

2) An understanding that projects still originate the same way: a problem, challenge or opportunity is identified, or a new idea to improve the business is suggested. Sources for suggestions range from front-line staff to objectives stated in the Enterprise's Strategic Plan.

3) The realization that dozens or more project ideas may be in play at any one time, but the average Enterprise does not have the resources to do them all; it must pick from the candidates which projects will get to proceed, and it must continue to do this as current projects are completed and resources are freed up.

It all boils down to best use of limited resources. The term that has emerged to describe all this is Project Governance.[13] The most common analogy used to describe this governance is "gating"; a number of things, like project ideas, enter into a process at its 'wide'

---

[13] In some ways, governance of IT has emerged a lot sooner than the newer Corporate Governance that deals with all aspects of a company's operations in order to meet with new compliance laws brought around by the Enron failure and the like. Many IT departments already recognized they had their own mess to deal with, hence Project Governance.

point, but only a small number emerge through the narrower gate at the end of the process. The projects that make it through the gate are initiated, the rest wait for another chance when more resources are available, or are eventually dropped from consideration.

It is the nature of IT projects that their size and cost start out small, but increase in size as they proceed through standard Analysis and Design tasks into actual development (commonly called Construction). As a result, a mature governance process will be comprised of several gates that continue after a project has been initiated. More will be known about the project as it approaches the next gate, where it is evaluated again to determine if it should continue. Sometimes a project will have made it through one gate but, after proceeding for a period of time, more information has been gathered and it is clear at the next gate that the original decision to proceed is no longer viable and the project should be stopped. This is NOT a project failure as described above. It is a success of the governance process to prevent wasting precious resources on continuing a project that will not be of value to the Enterprise.

The key question then is: what projects does the Enterprise consider to be most valuable? And the follow-up: how does it determine the value of any one project, so it can be evaluated against 'competing' projects? Again, I touched on this a bit in Chapter One, but here we will explore the value of projects in depth.

In private enterprise, the single common goal is sustained profitably[14], through a varying combination of revenue increases and cost reductions. Projects are often used to change how a company operates in the expectation that such change will deliver the desired revenue increase or cost reduction, and deliver it such that the value of the changes is not exceeded by the cost of the project itself.

---

[14] I emphasize "sustained"; any approach that maximizes profits in the short term, but damages a company's future profitably, works only for the sling-shot CEO who gets their bonus and then moves on.

So, we have two aspects of a project that will usually be used to determine its value:

1) Its impact on revenue or costs of the enterprise, commonly known as Benefits.

2) The Costs of carrying out the project (which some refer to as the 'investment')

Given these two dollar numbers, which is what they should always boil down to, you can then use them in one or more forms of what is commonly called a 'Cost-Benefit Analysis'. However, neither number just appears out of thin air, and any numbers you do come up with will never be exact, because estimating is involved

Lets' start with Costs (it's easier than Benefits, at least); essentially you need to define what resources, services and purchases will be needed when executing a project.

IT Project Costs

A typical IT project will involve IT people resources, of course; analysts, designers, programmers, testers, trainers, etc... The titles may be different at your company, but the people will be performing these roles. The question, of course, is how much of the valuable time of these people will be needed, and how much that does that time cost? This is when the estimating begins.

Estimating the cost of IT projects is a whole discipline in of itself. I highly recommend the writings of Vitalie Temnenco on this topic, such as "Software Estimation, Enterprise-Wide - Part I: Reasons and Means (June 2007), at

http://www.ibm.com/developerworks/rational/library/jun07/temnenco/index.html ,

where the author is described "an architect for the Ontario, Canada government's Workplace Safety and Insurance Board, where he provides architectural mentoring on implementation projects and helps teams embrace RUP and the Enterprise Architecture concepts."

In this article, he covers the most well-known techniques, classifying them as top-down or bottom-up, and continues on to cutting edge techniques like neural networks and Dynamics-based techniques.

My experience with estimating has led to always determining how accurate an estimate needs to be. When using cost estimates as part of a gating process, I find a reasonably supported estimate done in a short time will suffice. I have heard an initial estimating being referred to as "t-shirt sizing"; is it small or medium or large or extra-large, etc. Even this needs some context for a company, usually by classifying past project actual efforts the same way.

This supports the simple approach of "Is this new Project X the same size as a previous project we have carried out?" Assuming your company has kept the metrics about previous projects, and that is a big assumption, you can then extrapolate the size and cost of any similar new projects.

True, some one has to lay it on the line and decide if a new project is reasonably similar to previous projects, and the person doing that should probably define some assumptions about why they believe so. This allows the decision makers to agree with or challenge the assumptions as needed, until all are agreed on the assumptions and accept the resulting estimate.

If you have no metrics history to use, you may need to do some project planning to define the tasks likely to be carried out. Again, a whole other big discipline exists for project planning and management, and use of techniques of like Work Break-Down Structures (WBS). A simple web search or a visit to the Project Management Institute (PMI) website will get you started on that as needed. The only thing I emphasize in this approach is that as much as possible, people who would do the work should help in defining the necessary tasks, and then they most certainly should do the estimating of effort (usually in hours or days) of those tasks.

They know best what will be needed, and will make sure they are happy with the estimate because they will likely have to work to that estimate when the project starts.

In the end you will have a number of effort hours or days, and then you need an accepted price for an hour or day. Some shops will use a flat rate for all hours, while others will group the hours by role or seniority to get a range of rates. In either case, you multiply the hours/days by the price(s) and you have a cost. Other costs may be involved as well, especially one-time purchases of equipment or software needed by a project.

To go along with this cost, you will need an estimate of elapsed time for the project to execute and finish, because most benefits will not be realized until a project is over, and (later on) we will want to compute a present-value of future costs. More assumptions are needed; how many people will be assigned, what work can be done in parallel, etc. If you have used a project planning approach, you will have the advantage of defining many of these things already and will have come up with a project duration along with the project effort.

IT Project Benefits

Defining the benefits of an IT project is a different issue from defining costs; the latter may not be easy to calculate, but it can usually be done. Benefits, however, are usually in the mind of the people who want the project done, and generally are not easy to get defined and get a dollar value assigned to them.

In fact, the definition of benefits for IT projects does not exist as recognizable discipline. If you go searching for it, what you will always get is the answer that business sponsor/owner has to tell IT what the benefit is. If they can't reasonably describe and quantify a benefit, then the project will not happen.

In the early days of IT Projects, the stated benefit was usually the automation of manual effort; this was not always as simple to propose as it sounds, because automation usually was translated into reduced head count for the business. If the staff in the area affected by a project perceived it could lead to lay-offs, this could kill a project because you almost always need those people as the business experts[15] for the business scope of the project. I wrote many project proposals that had reduced manual effort as the prime benefit, but further described these savings as allowing the enterprise to take on more business without adding more people, or freeing up people to do new more valuable work for the enterprise; reduction in headcount was never mentioned.

However, automation of manual work as a benefit could usually be quantified in dollars in potential saved salary costs. The problem today, however, is that all the obvious automation projects have probably already been carried out at your company.[16] This leaves smaller or less obvious cost-cutting projects (taking orders on-line saves on paper costs...whoopee!), or, projects that are expected to increase revenue/income.

The question becomes: how much will such a project contribute to increased sales of products and/or services? This is difficult to predict, and most business people are leery of attempting to do so. Just like IT Project teams are held to a project estimate or be considered late/costly, business people who estimate revenue increases can be held to task if it is perceived that the expected increase did not materialize. An interesting corollary development is the increase in the number of companies that are evaluating projects some time after they complete (six months or so) to see if the promised benefits have been realized. This can make business people even more wary of putting their names to what is and should be treated as an estimate.

In the end, however, some dollar value of benefits needs to be proposed and agreed to, if a cost-benefit analysis is to be performed. All I can say here is that, like all estimates, stating your assumptions and having them agreed to as the basis of your estimate is crucial. If reality proves that one or more assumptions

---

[15] Often referred to as Subject Matter Experts (SME, pronounced "smee")

[16] If not, get to work!..but be careful not to "pave the cowpath" either.

turn out to false, then everyone involved in the project shares responsibility.

IT Project Cost-Benefit Analysis

Assuming you got through the rough stuff of defining costs and benefits, the analysis should be simple. What you want to know is if the benefits of the project will exceed the costs, and by how much. Since costs and benefits may be spread over long periods of time, Present Values of these amounts are also usually calculated to compare the amounts in "today's" dollars.

When I did my first Cost-Benefit Analysis for a major project, I had to work with an spreadsheet expert to do these calculations; now you can probably download something for free or a nominal fee that will do basic and advanced calculations. The key things these tools need is the two dollar values, cost and benefit, and the length of time of the analysis. The latter is usually defined by accounting standards at your company, and the most popular time periods used are three years and five years, often based around your company's depreciation procedures/periods.

Given that, you can usually get calculations like:
- Break-Even Point, the point in time when the benefits realized exceed the project cost
- Various rate of return and yield values, like IRR.

These calculations may be used to determine if a project passes a funding hurdle; it's not enough that a project makes money, it has to make more than investing the equivalent dollars of the project cost in securities or other investments.

After all this is done, a project can now proceed into the gating process to see if it has enough expected value to warrant its being initiated and carried out. Of course, if your analysis has determined already that the project does not have positive return or does not surpass the hurdle rate, you can stop now and move onto the next project idea. Determining that a project is not good for the business is just as valuable as finding those projects that are good for the business. Resources should not be wasted.[17]

---

[17] This is a good time to recommend that you never get too personally invested with a project, even with ones that were your own idea. If it doesn't proceed, you have to let it go. That's the way I have avoided emotional distress and ulcers in my career.

CHAPTER FIVE – Once a project is started, finish it.

No principle screams from the page to me than this one, yet rarely have I seen it implemented. This is a short chapter, as my recommendations back in chapter one for getting a current set of projects under control pretty much apply on an on-going basis as well. Given that, a discussion of this principle leads directly to the topic of company politics and its main driver, allocation and control of resources.

I have worked under various managerial styles, but it boils down to two approaches for me, integrated or divided. All enterprises of any size do need to be composed of many organizational units, but that is to divide up the people into manageable groups; it should not divide the enterprise into separate fiefdoms. Just think how many times you have seen or been part of a re-organization, and then think about how many times that has changed the actual work you or anyone else does; the latter adds up to just about nil.

Consider a complete enterprise, with all the usual line and staff functions[18]; ask anyone in that enterprise how it is structured to do its business and you will probably be shown an org chart. The usual hierarchy of boxes and lines, from CEO down to the base units, is the business graphic that is the oldest and most commonly used. However, why does it have to keep changing? That's because people are not robots, they need to be grouped in ways that maximize their contribution to the enterprise, while hopefully having job satisfaction and a boss they don't loathe; and since people come and go, and since people can change over time, any one instance of an organization (as represented by an org chart) will be become sub-optimal as time passes, so re-organization is needed, and that is a good thing if it re-energizes people and re-marshals the enterprise to be its most effective.

---

[18] Very large companies may actually contain several complete enterprises, for separate lines of business, or for different countries.

The problem is when management believes that the org chart at any one time also represents how the work gets done. Worse yet, they also use the org chart as the basis for changing/improving how the work gets done. This is the 'divided' managerial style I mentioned earlier, and it directly affects how the enterprise carries out projects.

Divided Management

At any one time, an enterprise has certain amount of capacity to implement change; the main numbers are how many people there are to do projects, and/or how much money is available to hire outside people to do projects. These numbers are a primary input to that common-place activity of annual budgeting/planning. Given Principle #1, these numbers are limited/finite, so managers need to decide how to best use them. In the divided managerial style, each major tree below the CEO on the org chart is allocated some portion of those numbers; if you have 10 people available for projects, the number used may be 120 person months. So, Sales is allocated 20 months, Operations gets 40, Finance gets 35, etc

Management may come up with what it believes are equitable/effective means of divvying up the number beyond just dividing it into equal units, but that is a sham; this is further reinforced by the sham idea that if each unit operates and changes successfully in of itself, then the total of all the units' success will equal the overall success of the enterprise. Does your company have internal charges between departments, often referred to as 'funny money'? Then your company is divided, because all that funny money means nothing to the bottom line of the enterprise.

A divided approach is a problem when projects are used to improve the business, because projects change the work, not the organization. Take an important and common business activity, order fulfillment. If you trace the work from when a customer first orders a thing or a service, to when its delivery is complete, many (many!) org units will be involved. So, if each unit independently attempts to change/improve that stream of work, they will either overlap with other units or duplicate what other units are doing without knowing it.

The main result for IT is that each org unit will want to use its allocated resources to get its own projects done. So, irrespective of their overall value to the enterprise, a number of projects will get initiated. This will result in overlap or duplication within the systems IT delivers, assuming the systems are delivered. IT management will be faced with conflicting demands on their limited resources, so only some sub-set of the projects will be proceeding while others wait for resources. This leads to projects stopping for a while when they get to a point where they need new types of resources, and then have to start up again when those resources eventually become available.

So, irrespective of the method used to divvy up project resources, the 'divide' approach produces an ineffective and wasteful projects environment. The solution to this problem is to move to an integrated managerial approach.

Integrated Management

An 'integrated approach' recognizes that an enterprise is a team brought together to operate a business, not a collection of independent fiefdoms; a CEO that recognizes and leverages this approach also knows that projects to improve the business belong to the enterprise, and almost always impact multiple organization units. Given this recognition, how an enterprise organizes its resources to carry out projects then will (or should) be tailored to the mix of people involved, just like any other aspect of organization. This could be anything, from ad-hoc teams to a full Project Management Office. Any good structure will do, as long as the enterprise view is maintained.

And that's all I have to say about that.

CHAPTER SIX – Specialize → each member of a team assigned to a project should do what they do best for the length of that project.

Subtitle: ...and why developing your own software may not always be the right thing to do.

This principle and principle #7 are probably the most likely to be 'controversial', if I am lucky enough to cause such a 'controversy'. As mentioned in the Forward, the debate these days is about the relative value of a 'generalist' versus a 'specialist'. The issue is not about the fact that there can be multiple roles on IT project, but whether you need specialists for each role to be effective, or if people can play many or all roles at different times and be effective (or be even more effective than specialists).

NOTE: The most common roles on an IT Project are usually agreed to be:
1) The Project Manager
2) The (Business) Analyst
3) The Designer
4) The Developer/Programmer
5) The Tester, or now known more as the Quality Assurance Analyst.
These are the roles I will be referring to in this and subsequent chapters.

If you were now expecting to read a rant about the perils of Agile Methods, I will have to disappoint you. I have indeed engaged in past virtual and face-to-face debates about Agile, usually spurred on by original claims that Agile projects "don't do Requirements" and/or Agile projects "don't need Business Analysts." As a practicing Business Analyst/Architect for over 20 years, 'them was fightin' words'. What I learned over time is that the above claims are not an accurate reflection of Agile based on the original Agile

Manifesto, and that there are various shades of what it means to be 'Agile'.

The one concept that has emerged and remained in play from Agile is that of the "Generalizing Specialist", a person who is probably most effective and experienced in one role, but can also adequately perform many roles on an IT project. A team of such individuals will bring all the expertise needed for each role, but no one individual has to depend as much on the work of others as input, since they can a lot themselves. Lastly, it is said of Agile that it does depend on a team of Generalizing Specialist for projects to be successful, but that they are hard to find.

From which a few things that can inferred:

1) An average company probably does not have any such rare people in its IT department.

2) Agile is also for delivering new software rapidly, but up to 75% of an average company's IT resources are spent on enhancements and fixes to existing systems. The remaining 25% that is actually spent on new software will also include the purchase and implementation of packages.

So, over 75% of the work going on in your IT shop cannot be improved by Agile software development, and virtually all your IT staff is not positioned to be successful with Agile, so how do you get all the rest of the work done? And how do you resource the IT department to be the most effective? The rest of this chapter deals with the first question, the next chapter with the second.

Teams

"There is no 'I' in Team"; who said that? Its been over-used, but it does obviously reflect the fact that an IT Project Team, like any team, succeeds or fails as a group, not as individuals; and it would seem the "IT Project Team" will be a structure that will continue to be used for some time to come.

So, what is a Team?

Definition:

1. side in sports competition: a group of people forming one side in a sports competition

2. cooperatively functioning group: a number of people organized to function cooperatively as a group

3. animals worked together: two or more animals worked together, especially to pull a vehicle or agricultural equipment

4. team of animals with vehicle: a team of animals and the vehicle harnessed to them

5. animals performing together: a group of animals that perform or are shown together

6. grouping of animals: a grouping of animals, e.g. a flock, brood, or herd

Source: encarta.msn.com

It's a bit unnerving that 4 of the 6 entries concern animals, but that's the English language for you. I like the following a bit better...

verb 1 (team up) come together as a team to achieve a common goal
Source: askoxford.com

... because it refers to 'a common goal'.

Why do we form teams? Because some goals cannot be accomplished by individuals; usually an individual does not have all the needed skills required to accomplish the goal, so other individuals that do have the skills are brought onto the team.

This has been true of human activity and culture for millennia; specialists have always existed that work together on teams, especially when specialty skills require great effort and experience to master. So when it was decided about 50 years ago that creating software required multiple skills, it was a natural progression that the team structure would be used.

However, is a team of specialists the best way to develop software? Because software development is so new, we tend to use analogies of other development/construction to help us understand what we are trying to accomplish; building a house is an-often used analogy.

The problem is that software is very different than building a house, an idea well described as follows:

> "The software-controlled electronic information system is fundamentally different from physical labor-saving devices such as the cotton gin, the locomotive, or the telephone. Rather than extend the ability of hand motion, leg motion, or the ability to hear and speak across distances, IT systems extend the capabilities of the mind—to think, to organize and disseminate information, to create."

> David R. Brousell
> Editor-in-Chief
> Managing Automation Magazine
> New York, October 2001

Because developing software is so different, is a team of specialists the best structure for software projects? This is truly what Agile is trying to figure out. I just don't know if they have got it right yet, as the nature of the software development process is still difficult to capture, CMMI and other approaches not-withstanding. Oh yeah, 75% of IT projects are not new software development, anyway.

In the mean-time, your IT department is chock-full of specialists. Winston Churchill is famously quoted as saying that "democracy is the worst form of government except all the others that have been tried." For right now, I will have to say this is also true of teams of specialists for IT Projects.

The Typical IT Project

Since most IT Projects today are not delivering new software, the nature of an IT Project and the growth of a team usually progresses as follows:

1) IT Project Idea is defined/derived.
Ideas can come from anywhere, but deriving them from company strategy and goals usually delivers the ones that will be perceived as most valuable.

2) One person is assigned to flesh out the idea so it can be evaluated by management.
That person is usually a Business Analyst (like me!) who takes what is known so far, and structures it into a Proposal format that is used to present the idea and allows comparison with other ideas/proposals in the same format. Some additional research or analysis may be needed, but you will always end up with a Proposal, which is then delivered into an evaluation process, like the Gating Process described in Chapter 4.

So, you start out with a 'team' of one; some companies like to assign a Project Manager as well, but there isn't really much to manage at this point.

3) The evaluation/gating continues to a point where a solution approach can be decided on.
This generally means the gathering and documenting of High-Level Requirements, essentially what the delivered result of the IT project will do that may make it valuable. "High-Level" means enough content to support the evaluation, but almost never enough detail that one could start designing the solution; the latter would take much more effort that would be wasted if the project does not proceed beyond the next gate.

There is no standard for what high-level requirements look like or how they are documented; the only thing that is important is that they are documented in an agreed way so they can be successfully communicated to all interested audiences. This is not easy, it is usually the main problem described in industry articles about why IT Projects fail so often; the requirements were incorrect. Lots of authors and gurus are available to help you with this (but I still may have to weigh in on this topic at some point...next book, maybe).

4) *Once an agreement is reached with the business on the High-Level Requirements, the Business Analyst and/or Project Manager investigate the possible solution approaches that the IT Project could use to deliver the desired result.*

I am still trying to find the original source for one of my favourite quotes that applies to IT projects: "Re-Use Before Buy, Buy Before Build, Build for Re-Use". However, Component Source (www.componentsource.com) uses the following version "Reuse Before you Buy before you Build™", trade-marked no less. Good for them, because I believe it is a powerful concept.

Re-Use before Buy:

In the IT marketplace, 'Re-Use' was a selling point of the first wave of Object-Oriented Development, such that software was to be built as components that could be used over and over again when creating new systems. I don't believe that ever really worked out on any grand scale for various reasons, including resistance from developers who want to build everything.

But, the concept ranges farther a-field than OO. For example, within a large company, especially one with many divisions and international locations, it is highly likely that the great new system you are proposing to build has already been built or bought and implemented somewhere else. A new project with a set of requirements should thoroughly search its company's portfolio of current systems to see if something similar already exists.

I am not saying this will be easy, as some companies' systems now number in the hundreds or thousands. It is in fact, one of the few things I use intranet searches for. If you can find something that meets 75% or more of your high-level requirements, it can't be ignored. Why? Because if you do ignore it, someone somewhere sometime will ask, "Why are we spending all this money on a new system when X Division has the same thing already?" Less cynically (or not), leveraging what your company already owns will deliver the end result to the business faster than any other approach and make you look like a star.

(Note that I still am talking about re-use, not 'sharing'. It may happen that you find an existing system that your business area can just start using, but that is extremely unlikely. There will be enough differences between the way your business area operates, and the way the current users of the system operate, that trying to rationalize the two to make the system truly shareable will be impossible.[19] Sharing had its own heyday as a concept as well, but it really only works in kindergarten... on the other hand, the whole Web 2.0 thing does indeed promote collaboration and sharing... a lot of sharing....)

The potential thorn in such re-use opportunities is that over the years systems have been built in many different ways, and such variations may impact any one system's potential for being copied and enhanced to meet another area's needs. You must engage designers and technical architects at this point to evaluate the potential effort to re-use a system in this way; the answer could be anywhere from small to huge, and you and your business sponsor need to know this before recommending/accepting re-use as a viable solution approach for your project.

Buy before Build:

In the evolution of anything, product or service, a point is reached where it is easier or cheaper or faster to buy it than make/do it yourself. Think of pioneers in the North American West who built/crafted almost everything they needed: house and barn, furniture, fences, etc. Today, if you have hand-made 'arts & craft' furniture from the 19th century, get thee to the Antiques Road Show to learn how much your windfall is worth.

---

[19] I am not saying here that the two business areas should actually be operating differently, it is likely that Process Improvement or BPR might find the differences don't actually add any value, but that is not for IT to trumpet on its own.

As I have and will continue to note, human beings have been building physical things large and small for millennia, and it is the nature of modern manufacturing and construction that these things are now made by companies for human beings to buy. Software is still very new, and it is not a physical thing, but we have already reached a point where you can buy software for almost any business domain or function[20].

How did this happen? Like anything new, building the first instances of software was hard work and usually took a long time to get it right, all making the effort expensive as well. However, once you have working software, you have a huge advantage over manufacturers of physical things; software can be copied instantly at virtually no extra cost beyond storage media. So, the more entrepreneurial among us thought "could I recoup some of my development costs, or even make a profit, selling this software to other companies?"

In many cases, the first main customers for a lot of software would have been direct competitors, so that did not make sense at the start. However, many new companies were often spun off specifically to sell some software, or the key developers left to form a company to quickly recreate and sell the same software. In other cases, very common functions soon appeared as software products, like General Ledger systems, that lots of companies could buy.

From then on, IT Projects were almost always faced with the "Build or Buy" choice. The resulting decisions were often couched in the culture of the company and/or its IT department. Some companies started buying packaged software early on, while many to this day stick to a "not built here" syndrome which denigrates anything from 'outside'. The decades have shown, however, that the average company will buy some software, or suffer greatly if it attempts to

---

[20] Here I am talking about business information systems, as opposed to shrink-wrapped products like MS Office.

always build its own software; only a few decidedly non-average companies can do that.[21]

However, buying software is not like buying a Chevy. If a car model only comes in a 4-door design, you can't ask the salesman to change it to a 2-door version. However, that's what happened often when software packages first entered the market. Early products were often based on one view of the business domain, the view of the people (or their company) who built it. So, packaged software was never a perfect fit to potential buyers. The value of buying, however, kept customers in the market, who were then faced with a new choice: change the software package to meet your unique requirements, or change how your company operates to match up with functions of the package.

Neither choice was appealing. Changing a package meant doing , analysis and programming, which is exactly what you were trying to avoid; change the package enough and you would also lose the ability to implement improved versions from the vendor. Changing your business to match up with the package... well, I don't think I have seen that ever happen, even when that was the plan to start with; something always turns up that the business can't live with, so the changes began.

But, the value inherent in buying over do-it-yourself was so great that vendors and customers survived the teething pains of packaged software. It was not long before the vendors figured out that software could be made more flexible to meet different customers' needs. User-defined fields were offered, and look-up tables for code descriptions, until it became apparent that packaged software had to be truly configurable, and this is where the word 'meta' started to appear, implying at least one if not many levels of generalization, so that customers could define their own business to the package through data, rather than change code.

---

[21] Again, I am talking about companies that use software to run a business, not software development companies, although I am sure that they buy commodities like GL systems as well.

Packages for Life and Health Insurance had to pick up on this fast, as nothing differentiates insurance companies more than their own unique products, so a general product definition function and data structure had to be offered. (Insurance is actually a lot like software, being intangible and subject to continuous change as actuaries come up with new twists.)

My own most recent experience has been with a Human Resources package. The unit I worked for within my multi-national employer was tracking employee sick time, vacation and overtime using everyone's initial favourite, Excel Spreadsheets. I was assigned to look for a solution, preferably something that could be acquired at minimum cost, and not use any (other) IT resources.

As a function, HR is common to all organizations, so I expected to find many packages to choose. I did, but not a huge number as a few vendors seem to dominate the time-attendance niche. Armed with Requirements I gathered from a representative group of Managers, I evaluated the available products and settled on one of the dominant vendors; their product was totally configurable from our perspective, could meet all our requirements, and was priced based on number of users so the cost was justifiable for the benefits we expected to get.

Now, configuration of a software system is really just another project for which it helps to have some experience. We decided to bring in two of the vendor's application consultants to do the actual configuration based on our requirements, which took about a week. Otherwise, I was the only person on the project, I used the IT department as my acceptance testers for 2 weeks, and then we went live.

(Ah, but doesn't that mean you are some kind of 'generalizing specialist'? Sure, I did the Project Management tasks, very little work there; and I did take on QA/Testing under the direction of our QA director. But, the system was small and the risk low, so we made it work. I would never claim to be an experienced Project Manager or Tester, and would not play those roles on larger, more mission-critical projects.)

Such configuration is the main feature of all the latest versions of good software packages, so now you don't have to make the choice about changing the software to meet your requirements; the software embodies such change.

Build for Re-Use:

OK, your project turns out to be one of the 25% or less that will need to build new software because nothing exists that you can re-use or buy.

5) *Once a decision to build is recommended and accepted, detailed requirements must be defined to the level necessary to design and develop the system...and then design, development, testing and implementation follow.*

As a concept, "Requirements" often seem to be the whipping-boy of the analysts or latest guru. The debate is not about Requirements as a 'concept' --- everyone agrees you need to know what is supposed to be developed! --- its about what is the best way to do it to ensure that the delivered software does do what the business needs. Projects delivering software that *doesn't* do what the business needs is still a common enough occurrence that a wide range of methods are still being used in attempt to solve this problem. This range is usually described as veering from formal, detailed analysis and documentation, all the way to the most intense forms of Agile methods. I believe there are also other axes of interest in play, notably code-generation from models, including older CASE tools or newer MDA approaches using UML.

In step (5) above, I do not lightly combine "*design, development, testing and implementation*" into one phrase; here is where the hard work gets done, where teams of multiple people/roles are involved. As I have proposed above, such a team at a typical company will be made up of specialists doing the various types of work, with a project manager to guide and control the work. This is where most

IT methodologies (like RUP[22]) provide the most detail and direction, and I do not intend to replicate that here or even recommend any one methodology; my only advice is use one that works for your company, and use it for a long time to maximize the return on your investment in that methodology; jumping from the latest hot thing to the next just costs too much in terms of the effort to change.

Given all that, I do believe its been clear for a long time that building things in pieces and sticking them together is the way to develop systems; consider the idea of high Cohesion and low Coupling in the original Structured Analysis and Design methodologies. Actually doing it so that these pieces of software, components being the most common name, can be re-used later on when constructing/assembling a new system, that's been harder to accomplish. Object-Oriented approaches were very big on this in '90s.

Can it be done? Is it being done? Object-Oriented was to deliver re-usable components, but the industry veered away from this goal as we moved from a CUA view of software to a web, browser-based view of systems. What the dozens of industry emails I get do tell me is that the new basis of re-use is Service-Oriented Architecture (SOA); instead of assembling software components into one whole system, you build a front-end (façade?) that invokes existing services, internal or external to your company. The services expose a public data interface and a description of its functions; you provide the data it requires, you get a result back. The travel industry was one of the first into external services, allowing systems to query different services in searches for flights, hotels and such that meet the provided criteria.

6) After the software is implemented, the original project is complete but the life of the software has just begun. Requests will be made to change or extend the system, and it may prove to have problems that are discovered after it has been in use for a period of time. This collection of changes and problems will likely lead to the initiation of that most common of IT projects, the Enhancement Release.

---

[22] Rational Unified Process

So, we have seen that many activities and steps in an IT project involve only one or two people, mainly the Business Analyst and sometimes a Project Manager. In the next chapter, let us consider what to do when multiple specialists work together.

CHAPTER SEVEN - One Architect/Analyst can generate enough work for two Developers and one Tester, structure your project teams in this ratio.

Your Business Analysts are the face of your project to the widest number of business people. It is their job to gather and consolidate all the needs and desires of the business --- the Requirements -- within the project scope, in such a way that the business people can understand and approve the result ("Yes, that is what I will pay for."), and that designers/developers can build the system that will meet those needs ("Yes, I can build something that will do this.").

If your project has relatively few types of business people who will use the system, and you are creating new software, especially when it is to support new functions such that the business does not yet know all of its needs, then by all means, gather the users, business analyst, developers and testers in a room and pound out the system in an agile, iterative approach. If the IT participants can perform multiple roles, then the ratio stated above does not matter.

However, I am betting that 75% to 90% of the time, your project will not look like this. Even if the user scope is narrow, it is still a common tug-of-war with business management to get users involved to the extent needed for agile approaches; or the knowledgeable users you need cannot be spared, and substitutes are provided who cannot give the team what it needs without checking with management or those other people you really wanted.

The other reason is that many projects have a wide number of potential users, with different (and maybe what looks like conflicting) needs, possibly spread out over multiple locations, perhaps literally spread around the world. So, someone has to deal with these complexities, and consolidate the results so that the appropriate solution can be delivered.

These days, that person is what is now commonly called the Business Analyst, charged with documenting the Requirements for the project. How Business Analyst's do that, and what the Requirement deliverable looks like and contains, is a topic for many books, and there are many, from Yourdon to Wiegers, so I will not write one today.[23] This should be a crucial part of the methodology you use in your shop, whatever the specific techniques or approaches it contains.

In essence, a methodology is used to make delivery of a solution faster, less work, and with a quality result. One of the ways it does this is by fostering communication between participants by providing a common language and structure. This is crucial for the business analyst's job, as their role is essentially communicative; their deliverables are intermediate, used to assist in creating the final delivered system. So, an important test of your methodology's effectiveness is if your developers can take the Requirements and build what they say is needed, without the developers having to spend more time trying to get any more detailed information that the Requirements did not contain.

When this is the case, my experience has shown that Business Analysts working with business people can, after completing an initial part of the Requirements, provide enough content to the rest of the team to keep two developers occupied with design and coding efforts, which is where the most time on your project will be spent. Separate testing of the new code produced by two developers will normally require one tester; many companies actually combine the Business Analyst and Tester roles.

I have found this 1-2-1 ratio to be a good rule of thumb. It may vary in some projects; if you have an experienced Business Analyst, they might be able to provide enough content for 3 or 4 developers, but not much more than that.

---

[23] Maybe tomorrow.

CHAPTER EIGHT - It's the Deliverable (that matters), not the Task

Delivering an IT solution is still a very complicated activity (becoming actively complex if it takes too long), and will likely be so for some time to come; so, it makes sense to simplify it whenever and as much as you can. This is where slavish adherence to a methodology can be counterproductive. Since IT projects are complicated, the idea of a defined process to carry them out emerged early on in IT history, giving us the "Methodology" as the cure for complication and the chaos common in projects.

First, having a common methodology for IT projects at your company is much better than not having one; CMMI statistics have made that clear. However, a methodology is a tool, not a religion to be practiced dogmatically. So, let us consider what a methodology offers as a tool and how best to use one.

There are different IT methodologies to choose from; the most common one is for developing new software, starting from nothing all the way to an implemented system. The number of different methodology products available, along with in-house variants, is beyond my counting, especially if you include the ones that have come and gone over the decades. Developing new software has always been the preferred/premier IT project, what most IT professionals will say they want to work on, many of whom were successful went on to offer their own methodology for sale(!).

I believe why we have so many to choose from is that developing new software is the most "blue-sky" of IT projects where, beyond conversion/transition from old to new, the methodology can purport how to do development with no attention to the specific environment or current systems being used at your company.

This is why I have virtually never seen a methodology for maintenance projects, beyond "find out what changes are need"

73

and "then make the changes." So, if you are doing IT maintenance projects, be aware that your new Software methodology may not be a big help for you.

The other major methodology you will see is the Project Management Methodology; IT is not the only discipline that uses a project structure to carry out work and produce a desired result, but there are so many IT projects in the 'world', using a PM methodology has emerged as a common approach in IT, driving the creation of the PMI and its PMM certification.

The key thing to note here is that you will use both your development/maintenance methodology and your project management methodology on one project. The former defines how to do the project, while the latter ensures it gets done, from inception to planning to execution to closing.

It is the planning of the project where the two intersect. The prime PM artifact for creating a plan is the Work Breakdown Structure (WBS), defining the tasks to be performed, dependencies between tasks, the people assigned to the tasks, and the effort and elapsed time estimates for the tasks. This can take a lot effort to create from scratch but, most development methodologies are precisely that; the set of tasks and such needed to produce the desired deliverable. So, plunk that set of tasks into your project's Gant chart, assign some real people, and off you go.

The problem is, methodologies strive to include all the possible tasks you might need in a systems project, but they (the good ones, anyway) don't mean to say that all those tasks are needed for every project; you are supposed to customize that set of tasks so that you end up with only the ones you really need.

The best methodologies even help you with this, offering customized versions of their task set depending on the type of IT deliverable you are going to produce. I have seen this for Data Warehouse projects, then for Website Development projects, and then for whatever came next. Information Engineering once even came with a Maintenance Methodology, although it was less about tasks and more about setting up a maintenance organization structure. (I wish I still had that one.)

Within your set of tasks, however, you need to pick up on the ones that actually deliver something useful, and weed out any "busy-work" tasks that don't contribute to getting the project done. The only deliverable of real importance is the final product. If you could just work immediately on creating that and produce a quality result, then a lot of this methodology "stuff" would not be needed. However, we found out early on in the IT discipline that you could produce something this way, but quality was likely not going to be attribute of the result. So, on came methodologies and the concept of the 'intermediate deliverable'.

The intermediate deliverables one usually sees in IT projects are:

- Scope Definition
- Requirements
- Design
- Code
- Executables

Methodologies may use different terminology, and most certainly break these down into subsets (like Functional versus Non-Functional Requirements). The key here is that things are delivered that can be commonly slotted into one of the above categories, and the real key here is that they should be something that another specialist will use as input to their assigned project tasks. Tasks that don't deliver something should be cut out of your task list, and even more importantly, tasks that deliver something nobody else uses should be cut out too.

So, if you are starting a project following your standard methodology, I recommend getting all potential team members together, especially those who don't come on until later in the project, and review what deliverables you might produce and determine if someone will use them, during or after the project (don't forget about training or support deliverables). This will give a clear set of deliverable-dependencies, and one can define the project's WBS around those dependencies; if you compare this to a previous project where this was not done, you will find your new project looks simpler and much easier to manage.

CHAPTER NINE - Leave a record of what you have done, so the project will not miss you if you leave...and Models are better than text

This is the other reason to have intermediate deliverables, to communicate what work has been done on a project, even if the person who did the work has left the project team.

..and people do leave. It's a natural step for IT people to move on to (perceived) greener pastures, so don't have unreasonable expectations about IT people; many have had jobs disappear from under them, and so are wary of company promises or homilies like "Our Employees are our greatest asset."

Given that the typical IT Project Team is a group of specialists, we need to know what each role will produce, and when. Let's revisit the list of intermediate deliverables:

- Scope Definition
- Requirements
- Design
- Code
- Executables

What format or structure would be useful for documenting each of these deliverables? As Principle #10 tells us, models are better than text.

Scope

Scope can be the trickiest thing to document in such as way that there is no misunderstanding among all the stakeholders and the project team; a poorly documented Scope can lead to questions down the line about why something is not being included, or why is something being produced that was not expected.

The basic artifact to use is the two part list: *In Scope* and *Out of Scope.* These can be presented one after the other or in a table with a column for each. The latter is effective in contrasting an item in one column with an item in the next column, like:

In Scope	Out of Scope
Current Customer Address data	Previous Customer Address(es) data

Another method is to use what is called a Context Diagram to define Scope, especially the expected scope of what the delivered system will do, and how it will interact with other items/systems in its environment. This usually means a box called the System in the center of a diagram, and a set of boxes around it showing systems and users that will interact with the System. Some methods will also open up the System box to show what components might be inside it. This method is useful when you are implementing a new system that will replace one or more existing systems (completely or partially) to show the impact and what the environment will look like; and it is close to being the first model you could create in your IT project.

In the end, a Scope Definition cannot be considered infallible; if you can capture the obvious Ins and Outs, and make sure you resolve any known conflicts about what is In or Out, that should minimize the number of downstream scope issues.

Requirements

Ah, Requirements; the part of the lifecycle where I mainly ply my trade. It is an aspect of systems delivery that has always seemed to be in flux, and sometimes under attack as unnecessary overhead. As I have said repeatedly, if you can put business people and IT developers in a room and start pounding out code that works and does what the business wants, power to you. For the rest of us, some record must be made of what is required of the desired solution.

Up first, do we all know what we mean when we say 'Requirement'? A good definition eluded me for a long time, such that I usually echoed the old US Supreme Court saying about pornography "I know it when I see it"; then I discovered the following definition:

> A requirement is a property that is essential for an IT system to perform its functions. Requirements *vary* (italics added) in intent and in the kinds of properties they represent. They can be functions, constraints, or other properties that must be provided, met, or satisfied so the needs are filled for the system's intended users (Roger Abbott 1986).

What this definition reminds us is that Information Systems are asked to do many different things; perform calculations, edit and store data, produce reports, support business process, enforce rules, etc. How do you capture business requirements that reflect such potential diversity?

Given that straight prose writing was always going to be too ambiguous for common understanding, many different structured written formats and diagrams/models have been used over the decades in best attempts to capture the elusive Information System Requirement. Much energy has been spent over those years by 'authorities' and 'experts' trying to impress various audiences that their specific format/diagram was the one true way to document requirements; heated arguments often ensued between competing camps as to why 'my way' is better than 'your way'.

This history, combined with the above definition of Information Systems Requirements, supports my thinking that no one format or diagram is sufficient to represent all Information System Requirements. Since information systems can do so many things, it is necessary to recognize that many means of representing the requirements are needed as well.

So, what should you consider using? In fact, many well-known types that have previously been used independently are good candidates; the set I currently use the most are:

- Declarative Requirement Statements
- Use Cases
- Data Models

- Process Models
- Business Rules

Declarative Requirement Statements

An occurrence of this artifact is a direct assertion of a "...property that is essential for an IT system to perform its functions." ; they are 'declarative' in that they do not imply any order or flow upon the information system..

The common structure is: "...the System must <specific statement>."

Variations on this structure include:

•   Referring to the 'Solution' instead of 'System', as an information or other type of 'System' is not always what is needed to meet the Requirements of the business. Business Analysis can identify the need for procedure or process change, for instance.
•   Variations on the verb 'must', such as 'shall' or 'will'; a 'must' statement is often interpreted as a mandatory requirement, while statements using other verbs mean the requirement is optional or 'nice-to-have'. If multiple verbs are used in a set of Requirement Statements, the specific meaning of the use of each verb should be clearly defined.

For example:

- "The System must provide security that a Manager can view salary data only for their own reporting staff."

- "The System must calculate the monthly payment for a loan application, given the Interest Rate, the Amount Borrowed, and the Number of Payments & Payment Frequency"

Such statements are usually part of a group of Requirement Statements, and can be documented at various levels --- from High-Level Requirements, documented first in a project to assist in scope definition and planning, to detailed statements used as input to Design and as the source of Test Cases.

Gathering these Statements can begin with a simple question to the business asking what they want the expected Information System to do. Their declarative nature focuses the business on 'what', steering clear of early assumptions about 'how' the system should meet those requirements. If a Business Analyst can document 10 to 25 Statements at the start of a project, the overall Requirements for the system will begin to take shape.

However, one should also expect that the number of Statements will grow as analysis continues, large enough to require some means of organizing them to improve their communication. The most common classification I have seen is functional versus non-functional, with the latter further sub-divided by types such as performance, security, legal, and more. These do tend towards how a system will operate or perform, which is fine, but that will still leave a Business Analyst with many Functional Requirements of what a system must do that need to be organized; can another artifact help?

Use Cases

Let us consider Use Cases, probably the currently best known and widest-used artifact in Information Systems development, both for Analysis/Requirements and Design.

I am a relative new-comer to Use Cases, after working in analysis and requirements through Structured Analysis and Design in the eighties, and Information Engineering in the nineties. I found one author's description of them almost aesthetically appealing, that each one is a case (or example) of the use of a system.

After that, I have seen many variations and permutations and various 'uses' of use cases; either that is a testament to their flexibility, or a condemnation of their vagueness. If you are new to Use Cases, be aware that different flavors of use cases are out there, being promoted and being used. When I am feeling the need for some rigor or consistency, I always go back to Alistair Cockburn (pronounced 'coburn') at http://alistair.cockburn.us/

Overall, I have seen and used two basic types of use cases:

1. A multiple-step interaction between Actor and System, which relates to user interface design, and capturing the required functionality the system must provide to support the interaction. I saw this a lot when working with co-workers who were OO designers and programmers.

2. A single step or occurrence format, where an Actor initiates the use case, which is provided some input and/or pre-conditions, and it executes a set of actions (calculate something, retrieve or store something else) that produces a result of interest to the Actor. (There may be multiple Actors, too.) The set of actions that are first defined are those that will normally execute, if no exceptions or other variations occur. I call this the 'happy path'.

   However, if it is known that one or more exceptions/variations from the 'happy path' could occur (due to certain input values or combinations of pre-conditions), these are documented as alternative paths. Creators of these types of use cases don't like to see path selection in their use cases, no "IF-THEN-ELSE" statements; use your alternatives instead.

Finally, both of the above types differentiate between the Use Case itself as the definition or template of the 'use of the system', and Scenarios, which are specific instances of the use case given one set of possible input values or pre-conditions; changing the input values produces another scenario, so a large number of scenarios could be defined for one use case, all of which will help the Testers of the information system develop test cases based on the use case(s).

As you might expect by now, I mainly use the second type of use case as part of documenting Information Systems Requirements. They are extremely valuable as a widely-accepted artifact for documenting the results of Analysis; anything that effectively assists in communicating Business Requirements to one or more audiences is something that should be used(!).

Now, they are not perfect, and they are not the ultimate artifact for documenting Requirements... they are only one artifact of many (five at my last count). One issue I had with use cases early on was identifying them in the first place: what was the scope of each use case? How many use cases do you need? There will definitely be more than one. What I can say now is that one way use cases can be identified is by there relationship with Process Models, which I describe later in this chapter.

However, once you do have a set of use cases defined that cover the scope of the business you are analyzing, you can also use them to organize the Declarative Requirements Statements. As I described earlier, I often start an Analysis effort by creating a list of High-Level Requirement Statements based on initial discussions with the business subject matter experts; if the these people want a new or enhanced system, they will tell you what they want from that system, which you can capture as Declarative Requirement Statements.

Once I have moved ahead to capture the necessarily detailed description of the business in use cases, I allocate those Declarative Requirement Statements to the Use Cases that will actually support the Requirements (if you end up with Requirements that don't match up to any of your use cases, you might be missing some use cases.) Detailed analysis will also support the definition of more Requirement Statements, again associated with particular use cases at a step level.

It might be argued that the detail provided in a use case supersedes the need for Requirement Statements, but I believe they still play an important role in communicating the essence of the use case; the Requirement Statements are often preferred by Testers as documentation of what they must test, and the Statements provide trace-ability from the Analysis through Design/Development to Testing.

So to this point, we have covered Declarative Requirement Statements and Use Cases, including how the two can be associated with each other... what about the data that is used in a Use Case, especially across many Use Cases for a domain?

Using Data Models for Requirements

Data Models are used to define the data needed for an Information system to use and/or control, and often form the basis for the definition and creation of databases. The most common format used to capture data requirements is the Entity-Relationship Diagram, which was most popularized by James Martin's and Clive Finkelstein's Information Engineering Methodology.

A web search on Entity-Relationship Diagrams or on Data Models will return thousands of hits, as I think that Data Models as a requirements artifact rival Use Cases in popularity. Here are two interesting links I found:

1) Data Modeling: Finding the Perfect Fit
An Introduction to Data Modeling
by Tim McLellan
Copyright 1995. All Rights Reserved.
http://www.islandnet.com/~tmc/html/articles/datamodl.htm

2) Applied Information Science
(Data) Modeling Methodologies
http://www.aisintl.com/case/method.html

In my use of data models for Requirements, the main component is the Data Entity, a subject of interest to the Business, associated by the business relationships between them. Each entity contains data items/attributes that relate to or describe the Entity. Each attribute belongs only to one Entity, so duplication of Requirements is

84

reduced.

Entity-Relationship data models are also commonly classified as 'Conceptual' or 'Logical', in that they are intended to communicate the data requirements of the Business. Such models can later be transformed into a 'Physical' Data Model that is used to design a database.

If a Data Model is used in conjunction with Use Cases, the latter's data items can be defined by a cross-reference to the Data Model. As a result, a data item used in multiple use cases will be defined only once, eliminating duplication and inconsistency.

Given integrated Use Cases and Data Models, what other requirement artifacts should be considered?

Process Models: Are they an Information Systems Requirement artifact?

The origin of Process Models as we see them today would likely make for an interesting academic paper --- systems and procedures and time & motion studies pre-dated information systems by decades. In any case, the profile of Process Models was certainly raised by Business Process Re-engineering; you had to define your Business Process before improving/re-engineering it.

However, as a format for documenting Information System Requirements, process models can have a negative impact on the resulting system. The process as it exists at the time of requirements documentation has often been 'hard-coded' into delivered information systems; when the process needs to change, the system cannot support a different process, and the business starts to adapt or create work-arounds to get the work done despite the constraints of the system.

This situation occurs frequently because it is not recognized that some aspects of the business are less stable than others. It has been shown that the process of a business, especially the order of separate steps, is the least stable aspect of a business; at the other end of the scale, the data items and their definitions as used by a business are the most stable aspect of that business. In between the two ends of the scale fall things like specific procedures (units of work) and business rules.

So, automation of the current business process should not be an Information System Requirement. In fact, generic process and workflow software products have been developed over the years to specifically support rapid change in process, adding or changing or re-ordering process steps as needed. These tools are enjoying a new profile as Business Process Management (BPM) products, as companies look for ways to integrate disparate systems, and vendors look for a front-end to SOA approaches.

Where Process Models can play a role in documenting Information System Requirements is to provide a context for Use Cases. Most steps in a process map will state that some work is done in that step, before the process flow continues; often this work involves use of an Information System, which can be documented as a Use Case. As stated earlier, the Use Case then provides context for Declarative Requirement Statements, as well as a cross-reference to data items and their definitions in a Data Model. In the end, knowing the overall process of the business or its subsets solves the issue common with Use Cases: how many do you need, and how do you know when you have enough... process context provides the answer.

Just a few years ago, this would have been the last 'artifact' that I would have discussed. However, a new emphasis on methods and formats for documenting Business Rules has recently emerged.

Business Rules

As a concept, Business Rules are not new, to the Business or IT; what is new is the focus on separating them from other forms of documentation so they can better defined and managed.

Business Rules are similar to Process Models/Maps in that they are subject to more frequent change than other aspects of the business, frequently enough that if rules are hard-coded in an information system, the effort and elapsed time to change the system can be too large to be tolerated by the business over time. So, just as generic Process 'systems' are emerging to support rapid process change, so are Business Rule Systems products that support Business Rule Management independent of the information systems that use them.

What is a Business Rule?

"A business rule is a statement that defines or constrains some aspect of the business. It is intended to assert business structure or to control or influence the behavior of the business. The business rules that concern (an Information Systems) project are atomic – that is, they cannot be broken down further." ... *from "Defining Business Rules ~ What Are They Really?", Copyright ©2001, the Business Rules Group.*

I would add the word 'declarative' to the definition, as in "a business rule is a declarative statement that defines...", emphasizing that Business Rules do not imply a process, procedure, flow or other 'system' structure. If Business Rules are separately defined and managed, they can then be used as needed by any process/procedure/flow that needs a rule's guidance or constraint.

Some examples of business rules include:

- The insurance coverage for a 10 year Term Life Insurance Policy must be $50,000- or higher.

- Premiums paid by direct debit must have a monthly payment frequency.

- A person may be the life insured on multiple policies, but only if the total coverage of all the policies does not exceed $1,000,000-.

To ensure that Business Rules are meaningful and clear, they are based on a defined set of 'Terms and Facts', which are used as the language of the Rules. Terms from the above examples include insurance coverage, premium, policy, and person. An example of a fact would be "a person may be the life insured on multiple policies ": it's when you add the constraint "but only if the total coverage of all the policies does not exceed $1,000,000-" that you have a rule, using   that   fact   and   the   relevant   terms.

Defining terms and facts can also be seen as a role of an Entity-Relationship Data Model, such that the Entities/Attributes and Relationships of such a Data Model can readily be used as the Terms and Facts for defining Business Rules. The two types of models are different in many ways, but they are similar enough that if you have one, you can easily use it to drive the creation of the other.

Integrating Requirements Artifacts:

To recap we have covered all the Requirements formats that I commonly use:

· Declarative Requirement Statements
· Use Cases
· Data Models
· Process Models
· Business Rules

I have touched on some aspects of how these formats can be inter-related and integrated. Let's review all these formats and add some more aspects of integration.

In summary:

- Process Maps identify all steps of a process, and a Process Step can indicate when a Use Case is used in the Business. One Use Case may be used by multiple steps.

- Use Cases can include one or more Declarative Requirements for the Information System/Solution. Each Requirement Statement is allocated to one and only one Use Case.

- A Data Model will document all data items used within the scope of a set of Use Cases, and is cross-referenced in the Use Case for the data items used by the latter. So, a data item is defined once

Cascade

but can be used in multiple Use Cases.

- Business Rules can also be documented across the scope of the Business being analyzed, including both the set of Use Cases and the overall Process Map; a Business Rule may be invoked at different points and times within Business Operations. Use to date has shown they can then best cross-referenced in:

> - The Use Cases whose execution is impacted by one or more Business Rules

> - Process Maps at Decision Points, as Business Rules may play a role in deciding which path within a Map should be followed in any one execution of the Process

The integration described above can be illustrated in the following diagram:

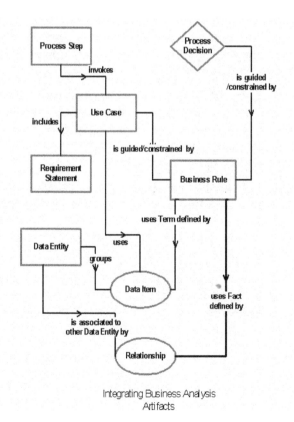

Integrating Business Analysis
Artifacts

89

It is at this point where the cross-requirements traceability of this level of integration can be seen to support Impact Analysis of potential Requirement changes; for example, when a change to a Business Rule is being considered, the measure of its potential impact can be gauged by tracing to all the Use Cases and Process Decisions that the rule currently constrains.

Used together as an integrated set, I find these Requirements artifacts present a comprehensive set of Information System Requirements. However, Requirement Artifact formats and artifacts come and go, so in the long run, it is not as important to use the 'best' Artifacts, as it is that you recognize you will need multiple types of Artifacts, and they should be integrated to reduce duplication, and present multiple views of the same Business domain.

Postscript: even while writing this material, the discipline continues to evolve, especially for Business Rules. The need for flexibility in changing rules, and the potentially very large number of rules a company may have, have changed the view on Rules as a Requirements to being an aspect of systems that must be managed by the business, like data managed in databases, and processes managed in BPM tools[24]. So, we know see the emergence of Business Rules Management Systems (BRMS), which support capturing rules declaratively in a model, which can then be implemented by a Rules Engine, a platform that accepts request for decisions and returns results to calling systems or BPM processes.

The result is that the nature of application systems is changing, where the more volatile parts of a system have been factored out of code, with the remaining functionality being very stable; i.e. business changes that used to mean code changes in the past now can be managed by the combination of DBMS, BPM, and BRMS.

---

[24] Hindsight helps us see that Business Rules are not System Requirements, Rules exists whether you have a system or not. The requirement is for systems that support Business Rules.

Pure code that remains focuses primarily on the user interface and other means of acquiring data, and the storing of that data in the DBMS. This is accompanied by any complicated manipulation of data that code crunches best, from math calculations to beating chess grand masters.

At this point, however, we have a definition of what a solution (some combination of management systems and code) should do, but not how; that is the realm domain of Design.

Design

How do you design something you cannot physically touch? Consider what the following writers say about information systems and software:

> *"We need to know the fundamentals and formulas by which software behaves. What are the laws and principles we can count on in creating it? The problem is that software is not a thing, not a preexisting phenomenon of the universe; it's a product of the human imagination."*
> *Scott Rosenberg, talking about his book "Dreaming In Code: Two Dozen Programmers, Three Years, 4,732 Bugs, and One Quest for Transcendent Software (Crown, 2007)", at http://www.cioinsight.com/article2/0,1540,2079462,00.asp?kc=C OQFTEMNL101807EOAD*

> *"The software-controlled electronic information system is fundamentally different from physical labor-saving devices such as the cotton gin, the locomotive, or the telephone. Rather than extend the ability of hand motion, leg motion, or the ability to hear and speak across distances, IT systems extend the capabilities of the mind—to think, to organize and disseminate information, to create."*
> *David R. Brousell*
> *Editor-in-Chief*
> *Managing Automation Magazine*
> *New York, October 2001*

So, beyond issues of response time and at least minimal effective use of ever cheaper and faster computer hardware, the designer of an information system faces no serious natural constraints. This is a double-edged sword, as almost any design approach has a good chance of producing a working solution, but may suffer afterwards if no one else understands the approach (and the code it produced), or the solution cannot be changed easily, or any other maintenance horror stories you know of.

So, just like the Requirements discipline has featured different and competing approaches, so we have seen the same in Design; what has emerged over the past 20 years is the acceptance of Object-Oriented (OO) and the Unified Modeling Language (UML) as the most recognized Design approach for Information Systems to be coded. Your designers/developers may or may not be using UML, but they know what it is. I will not attempt to describe UML here, as www.uml.org gives you the Object Management Group (OMG) standard for UML, and a simple web search will find many books and other resources to help one understand and use UML

As a Requirements Analyst, I find the most common cross-over point from Requirements to Design is the Data Model and its influence on UML's Class Diagram; they both speak to the concepts/classes/entities of interest to the enterprise. Their structures will be different, as data models concern definitions of data 'at rest' (leading toward design of the database), while class diagrams concern data ' in motion' or ' in memory', i.e. how data is used in the execution of a system function, perhaps for as little time as a nano-second. The rise of UML is more recent than my own early experiences with system design and coding, but I do understand that all other aspects of UML hang off the Class Diagram.

As mentioned earlier, the interesting thing now is how much less of a functional information system needs to be designed these days. Database Management Systems have been around long enough that UML doesn't really deal much with the modeling of what it calls "persistent data", i.e. data that continues to exist after the execution of a program. Increasing use of BPM and BRMS tools mean that processes and rules do not need to be implemented in code, so the key design scope is on the components that gather and use data, i.e. make information.

Code

I have coded, been paid to do it; I know that creating code to solve a unique problem or offer new service is exhilarating. I also know that the majority of coding I did was to copy an existing program and modify it in some way to do something the original didn't; that type of coding was not so exhilarating.

This common situation led to two main outcomes:

1) Object-Oriented Design, where-in code that performed a certain function would be created once and shared or re-used as-is fro the rest of time.

2) Generation of code from models (especially data models), using tools that were first called Computer Assisted Software Engineering, or CASE tools.

Both of these approaches worked, but neither of these impacted IT as expected by their originators. Re-use of Objects has always faced resistance from programmers who wanted to code, not re-use; and their employers often rewarded programmers on the same basis, so re-use was never viewed as valuable.

CASE tools also faced resistance from programmers, but were being adopted by companies to augment their limited numbers of programmers. Many frequent-flyer systems still in use today can trace their origins back to TWA's system developed using the IEF tool; given that it was generated from models, they could sell the models to other airlines who could then generate code for their own environment[25].

---

[25] THE EMERGING USE OF APPLICATION TEMPLATES

However, two more things happened that killed CASE:

(1) IBM's ill-advised attempt to dominate the market with its AD-Cycle approach for integrating different CASE tools. It failed miserably, tainting all CASE tools as failures as well.

(2) The arrival of big, new ERP products like SAP killed a lot of in-house development, CASE or not, when these products were sold as the quick way to replace a company's systems.

Neither approach to producing code totally disappeared and, in fact, have merged in the new development approach called Model-Driven Development/Architecture (MDD/MDA). The models being used are UML diagrams, which emerged from the OO camp. MDD/MDA has not taken off yet, facing the same resistance as older approaches to reduce/eliminate coding by hand, but no less a player than Microsoft is getting behind it with its 'Oslo' approach.

In the mean-time, most code is still created by programmers the 'old-fashioned' way, which can still lead to code that cannot be understood by anyone except its creator, who probably moved to greener fields leaving the mess behind. Coding standards are used to prevent this problem, and even I was encouraged to heavily 'comment' my code back in the day. Clear links/references to the Design can also help... until code generation eventually takes over.

John F. Rockart
J. Debra Hofman
December 1992
CISR WP No. 250
Sloan WP No. 3523-93

CHAPTER 10A - Partition large projects into 3 month phases, that is the longest period you can plan for without the chance of significant change to priorities, resourcing, etc.

Speed and Agility are the by-words these days, and why not; Slow and Clumsy would be tough to sell.

What experience has showed us that Slow is really bad for IT projects; if your projects are taking 6 to 12 months or more from initiation to delivery of solutions, it is undisputed that the world will have changed enough that what is delivered will not match up with what is really needed at that time.

On the other hand, there is a cost to being too fast, and it is not necessarily to the detriment of the quality of the delivered solution. Small increments delivered quickly still may need to be integrated into a larger whole before it can perform a complete enough function to be useful to the business. There is also a cost to change, since implementing new software requires training of users, changes in procedures where the new system is used, etc.; do this too often and your company will be expending more effort on changing than on the actual work that makes money.

What I have seen is that 3 month cycles are the balance between too slow and too fast. Changes will still happen within that cycle, but of a scale that should be manageable most of the time. This includes changes in the business need, and changes to the project such as team members leaving for other pursuits.

Another good reason is that most businesses operate in 3 month /quarterly cycles, better known as the "Q's": Q1, Q2, Q3 and Q4. Simply adopting some business terminology and process to IT can only improve the partnership between the two parties.

CHAPTER 10B – Within the three month phase, parcel work into two-week periods...

... analyze for 2 weeks, then design and develop for 2 weeks (2 developers), and then test for 2 weeks. When the first 2 weeks of analysis is done, start the next two weeks of analysis in parallel to the design/development; carry on in cascading 2 week periods until the entire project scope has been addressed.

Within a project schedule, two weeks is a critical number. Breaking down the work into tasks shorter than two weeks can lead to micro-managing; tasks longer than two weeks can run out of control, or stagnate, for too long before it is apparent they are in trouble.

What if you have a specific piece of work that only takes a day or two? Bundle it with other tasks that overall bring the elapsed time to two weeks. However, be flexible as well; I am just saying that two weeks is an optimum elapsed time to work with, and tasks that take more or less should be analyzed to determine why. If a specific task does need a different elapsed time, accept it but keep an eye on it too.

Another set of numbers I have seen on most projects is the percentage split between project phases/roles, as follows:

- Requirements   25%
- Design and Build[26]   50%
- Test   25%

These percentages support my project structuring of one Business Analyst, two Designer/Developers, and one QA Tester. This 'group of four' can be a basic building component for project teams. Given an early partitioning of project scope into cohesive/de-coupled

---

[26] Is there a common percentage split between Design and Build(code)? Perhaps, but I am not sure if the two are always as distinct as stated here.

portions, multiple groups of four can be assigned to a project, sometimes in parallel or at least with some overlap.

And, as described in chapter 7, start off with just your Business Analyst for two weeks, and they will produce an intermediate deliverable of value to Designers/Developers, the description of what the solution must provide. This drives the two weeks of subsequent design/development work that produces the next intermediate deliverable, draft or un-tested code[27]; the latter drives the two weeks of QA testing, producing a final deliverable of code ready to be integrated in a quarterly release.

Meanwhile, the cycle has started again after the initial two weeks of Business Analysis work. Intermediate deliverables quickly flow through the solution delivery process, like a cascade of water through a chute or rapids to a pool below. The pool builds up with increments of code, ready to be released to production on a planned schedule.

---

[27] I bundle initial (unit) testing by the developer into the middle 50% of effort. Testing after that will be for integration, volume and requirements-met testing.

CHAPTER 11 – Given many medium to small software Deliverables, use Architecture to manage and integrate the Deliverables into a complete system.

In this principle, I am speaking to the use of Architecture right down at the project level. Since this book is still primarily about information systems, two Architectures are always of primary interest to me: Data and Function. Remember, "Data + Function = Information".

> Sidebar: time for my two favourites 'famous quotes' about Information:
>
> "As a general rule the most successful man in life is the man who has the best information."
> Benjamin Disraeli
>
> "Information is like eggs, the fresher the better."
> George S. Patton

If you are fortunate, you may already have at least a Data Architecture available for your company; any company with a serious investment in relational databases probably has some Entity-Relationship models defined that were use to design those databases. If so, there will be Data Base Analysts (DBA's) working for you that care for these databases and the models, and there may even be Data Analysts (DAs) who created the original ER models at a conceptual or logical level. Even if the models are very physical and with strange short forms for names and such, these can still be a starting point for retrofitting a Data Architecture for use in IT projects.

In the end, you need a set of Entity Types and their relationships required by the scope of the system, and the functions that Create, Read, Update and Delete entity occurrences, documented in a

CRUD matrix. In a very pure approach, 'Update' and 'Delete' are actually just variations on 'Create': systems should never delete data unless physical limits are reached or retention/privacy polices require it; that way all data collected is always available... and updating an existing occurrence of an entity means that you lose the fact that the original data ever existed, so you should create a new version of the occurrence with the changed data, and mark the original occurrence as no longer effective, or that it has been 'logically deleted' with a status value.

Note that documenting 'Read's is not crucial, as reads will not impact how a system is structured. However, they do show what parts of a system need data created by other parts of a system, which drives out your logical build sequence, i.e. you have to build the Create functions before the data they create can be used by other functions. However, we are not talking about reading data created by a system for Reporting/Warehousing or Business Intelligence. To those capabilities, your information system is a data source only, but it certainly helps if the system provides valid data to those external capabilities.

Function/ Data	Accept Order	Fill Order	Ship Order	Validate Shipment Arrived	Bill For Shipments	Receive Payment for Shipments
Customer	R					
Order		C	R			
Shipment			C	U	R	R
Invoice					C	R
Bank Account						R
Bank Deposit						C

Sample CR(UD) Matrix

Given these core Data and Function Architectures, other parts of the Zachman Framework can be added on to further document the overall Business Architecture needed to direct how systems are to be developed.

For example, consider Where/Location:

Function/ Location	Accept Order	Fill Order	Ship Order	Validate Shipment Arrived	Bill For Shipments	Receive Payment for Shipments
Sales Office	X			X		
Warehouse		X	X			
Accounting					X	X

"X" marks the intersection of a Function and where it takes place.

Next, Who/People or Role:

Function/ Role	Accept Order	Fill Order	Ship Order	Validate Shipment Arrived	Bill For Shipments	Receive Payment for Shipments
Salesman	X			X		
Warehouse Stocker		X	X			
Accountant					X	X

"X" marks the intersection of a Function and who performs it. This documentation can also be expanded to include When (such as Billing Cycle) and Why (rules for accepting an Order).

Given this overall Architecture, each increment or release of a system can be defined by which matrix intersections it includes, which also indicates which intersections remain for future releases.

CHAPTER 12 – Conclusion(s)

And that's it! ...at least for the time being. More good practices will reveal themselves over time, usually from hard-earned experience. For now, just remember:

1. *There is always more work to be done than people to do it.*

2. *Projects change the business, so know the overall business first.*

3. *Use an overall Architecture to describe the business, before and after projects.*

4. *Pick the right project(s) for the business.*

5. *Once a project is started, finish it.*

6. *Specialize – each member of a team assigned to a project should do what they do best for the length of that project.*

7. *One Architect/Analyst can generate enough work for two Developers and one Tester, structure your project teams in this ratio.*

8. *It's the Deliverable (that matters), not the Task.*

9. *Leave a record of what you have done, so the project will not miss you if you leave.*

10. *Models are better than text.*

11. *Partition large projects into 3 month phases, which is the longest period you can plan for without the chance of significant change to priorities, resourcing, etc.*

12. *Within the three month phase, parcel work into two-week periods; analyze for 2 weeks, then design and develop for 2 weeks (2 developers), and then test for 2 weeks. When the first 2 weeks of analysis is done, start the next two weeks of analysis in parallel to the design/development, carry on in cascading 2 week periods until the entire project scope has been addressed.*

13. *Given many medium to small software Deliverables, use architecture to manage and integrate the Deliverables into a complete system.*

Request For Feedback

I would like to hear what your experiences are in multi-project environments, and if you have suggested amendments to my practices, or brand new ones to offer the world; send them to me at dwwright99@hotmail.com, and presuming future editions of this book will be forthcoming, you may see your name in print.

A few websites are also being developed for Cascade, starting at
http://dwwright99.iwarp.com/index.html
 and
http://www.beep.com/members/dwwright99/
; perhaps Cascade will move to its own domain at some point.

→ In the meantime, visit early, visit often.

David Wright

Index

Cascade

Cascade